Albion Winegar
Tourge

e

The war of the standards

coin and credit versus coin without credit

Albion Winegar
Tourge

e

The war of the standards
coin and credit versus coin without credit

ISBN/EAN: 9783744739559

Printed in Europe, USA, Canada, Australia, Japan

Cover: Foto ©Suzi / pixelio.de

More available books at **www.hansebooks.com**

THE WAR OF THE STANDARDS

COIN AND CREDIT

versus

COIN WITHOUT CREDIT

BY

ALBION W. TOURGÉE

Author of "A Fool's Errand," etc.

———

G. P. PUTNAM'S SONS

NEW YORK   LONDON
27 WEST TWENTY-THIRD STREET   24 BEDFORD STREET, STRAND
The Knickerbocker Press
1896

CONTENTS.

PAGE

I.—THE CURRENCY ISSUE OF COMMANDING IMPORTANCE . 1

II.—WHAT IS THE ISSUE? . 10

III.—AN OLD, OLD STORY 18

IV.—THE WORLD'S VERDICT 25

V.—MONETARY EXPERIMENTS . 36

VI.—"THE CRIME (?) OF 1873" 42

VII.—DEPRECIATION OF SILVER 49

VIII.—A NEW ECONOMIC LAW 56

IX.—THE DECLINE OF PRICES 63

X.—"VALUE," "EQUIVALENCY," "MONEY," "CREDIT" . . 73

XI.—NATIONAL CURRENCY AND NATIONAL CREDIT . . . 82

XII.—TERMINAL LEGAL-TENDER CREDIT-MONEY. 98

XIII.—THE RESULTS OF FREE COINAGE OF SILVER. 105

XIV.—CURRENCY AND PROTECTION 118

XV.—THE RICH AND THE POOR . 126

THE
WAR OF THE STANDARDS:

COIN AND CREDIT
versus
COIN WITHOUT CREDIT.

I.

THE CURRENCY ISSUE OF COMMANDING IMPORTANCE.

WITH the advance of civilization the interdependence of man upon his fellows, both individually and collectively, comes to be a matter of constantly-increasing importance. The closer lives approach to other lives the greater the opportunity both for conscious and unconscious good and evil.

Exchange is the greatest of all the means by which society exercises its mighty power over the individual. The man who neither buys nor sells has little power, and is subject to few influences. The more a man sells or buys the more dependent he becomes on others. Civilization multiplies his wants, his desires, his interests, his opportunities. Every need opens a door by which another enters into his life. Every time he buys or sells, the other party to the transaction does something to condition his life, and is in turn the recipient of influence from him. The instrument by which this influence is chiefly exerted is currency ; since by this the greater part of all exchange is effected. If a man has to buy what he eats, what he wears, what he occupies, what he uses, what he enjoys, then money becomes to him as the breath of life to his nostrils.

To the savage and the "hobo," who live on what nature supplies or man gives, money is of little consequence. But to him who gives something for everything he receives, who pays for whatever he has, by giving something in exchange, money is the most important thing in, life, because it represents all that supports, adorns, and makes life enjoyable to the individual or useful to others.

Civilization, through the contiguity of man with man which it compels, not only conditions life with the dollar-mark, but makes a thousand things which were without price, attainable only by the payment of money. To primitive life the sun furnishes light, the streams and springs water. The forest and the desert need no roads, man's own limbs furnish locomotion. Civilized society requires roads, streets, cars, lights, a water supply, railroads, telegraphs, telephones—and for all these some one must pay. Society supplies the greater portion of them, but the individual must pay society for the privilege of using and enjoying them. Toll is levied at every turn of the path of civilized life. The physician demands a fee at the entrance gate ; the teacher at the door of the school-house ; the minister at the marriage altar ; the undertaker at the grave. All that we eat, all that we wear, nearly all that we drink, must be paid for. A price is set upon half that we see, upon the streets we walk, and the means of transit and communication we use. There is a price-mark on every necessity of life, every luxury, and every privilege. The law, the courts, the police, the government that secures them to us—all these cost money ; for all of them society must pay and the individuals who compose society must reimburse it for the outlay. The dollar is the foundation-stone of civilization. Salvation may be free, but a price is set on all the means of grace—the church, its priests, its altars, all its agencies. Even the " Salvation Army " and the deeds of charity which good men and women do for their fellows—for all of these some one must pay. Man is no longer saved by faith alone, for money is required to make faith effectual. Cash is essential to make the doctor's prescription available, the lawyer's advice of any value, and to give effect to the prayer of faith. We say the air is free, but there is no place in all the civilized world where it can be breathed without somebody paying, in some way, for the privilege.

Is it any wonder that every one should have an interest in that which measures all need, grants all privilege, opens every gate of opportunity, gives effect to aspiration, and is the condition of all enjoyment and usefulness?

The character and efficiency of the currency, which is the medium by which all exchange is effected, is the most vital and universal question that can be presented to civilized man, because it colors and conditions every moment of his life. Production is a matter of vast importance ; commerce a thing of absorbing interest. The conditions that affect labor and its employment are of the highest interest to all, because labor is the chief element, both of production and of commerce ; but the character and efficiency of the currency is of pre-eminent importance to each and every one, because it is the universal measure both of production and of consumption—of labor, use, and enjoyment. No other social or political question, save only liberty, can approximate it in importance ; and only religion and love can exceed it in influence on human destiny. To touch it is to touch the life of every man, woman, and child in a civilized community.

Because the currency measures all material things that enter into the universal life, it is easy to perceive the truth of the seeming paradox, that *he who has the least of it is most concerned as to its character and quality.*

The man who handles little money consumes his whole store every day. It measures his daily bread, his health, his strength, his leisure, his happiness, his value to himself, to his family, and to society. If we reduce the purchasing power of the money he receives, which is now just sufficient for his needs, he must do without just that much of what is essential to his vitality and value. Take away ten per cent. of the purchasing power of the currency and you take away ten per cent. of the manhood and womanhood of half the people of the United States, and increase thereby the burden of poverty, crime, and vice. The man who suffers want is thereby the more inclined to be a criminal. The woman that cannot earn a livelihood honestly has the greater temptation to obtain a dishonest one. So the currency question is one of morals as well as comfort and happiness, to those who have only enough. To the man who has more than enough for to-day, the quality of the currency is a matter of less moment, since its lack of purchasing power affects only his surplus. To the man who has great wealth, it is a matter of comparatively little consequence; since at most it only reduces his superfluity. Ten per cent. shrinkage only takes a dime off the laborer's daily wage ; but that means a loaf out of his daily bread. From the man who has a million dollars it would take away a hundred thousand dollars ; but he would have nine hundred thousand left —more than he can consume or even use, except for mere gratification of his desires. What then is the ratio between the interest which the poor man has in the quality of the currency, and the rich man's interest in it ? What comparison shall adequately express it ? It is as the diamond to the dust on the jewel-cutter's tool. A yard cut from a roll of ribbon is a trifle ; an inch taken from a man's collar means suffocation.

But it is claimed that if the *purchasing power* of the

present currency should be reduced by the free coin-age of silver, say one-tenth or even one-half, the man who has now but little money, who day by day consumes his daily wage, will get a great deal more, and so be enabled to buy perhaps two or three times as much of the things he needs.

This is a fair proposition and a plain one. It means an exchange of less for more. If it is a correct hypothesis, everybody should favor the change. Even if it would give to the poor man more and to the rich man less of purchasing power than he now controls, everybody ought to favor it. The rich man could afford to be not quite so rich in order to see all his poor neighbors more abundantly provided with the necessaries of life and its most important comforts. There may be millionaires who would rather hold all they have than lose a tenth in order to improve the general condition one fifth or even one half; but it is not probable there are many such. Men may not be willing to give much to charity, because they say to themselves : "What I may give will go but a little way"; but there are very few men who are even moderately rich, who would not be willing to see their superfluity greatly lessened in order to increase in like ratio the ability of *all* those who have not enough.

In like manner, there are men no doubt who have barely enough to live, who would be willing to lose a part of this in order to see the rich stripped of their superfluity. Envy is just as base a sentiment as greed.

Neither is a good criterion of individual or public duty, and neither constitutes the general impulse of any modern community. The average civilized man likes to see others prosper as well as prosper himself. The swine is not the true emblem of Christian civilization.

So, if the proposed change will increase the ability of those who have not enough to acquire needful comforts, though it should not proportionately increase the superfluity of those who have more than enough, or even if it should increase the ability of the poor to gain creature comforts and not enhance the superfluity of the rich at all, rich and poor alike ought to heartily favor the change. And no doubt a vast majority of both classes would, if they could only be made sure of such result or even of its reasonable probability. The claim of the advocates of the free coinage of silver is that it will do *at least one of these things.* If it will they ought to win. But suppose it should not, and instead of enabling the man who is now able to get barely enough, to earn more, it should reduce both his sufficiency and the rich man's superfluity—or reduce the present ability of the man who with difficulty gets enough without impairing the superabundance of the rich, what then ? A rich man can afford to gamble. He stakes only his superfluity against the chance of greater gain. But when the poor man gambles he stakes his manhood, his strength, the happiness of his wife and the hope of his children. If he loses, he has lost that which is beyond price.

The currency issue of to-day is simply this :

The advocates of the unrestricted coinage of silver claim that the adoption of that policy at this time by the United States, would better the conditions of those who are now able with difficulty to gain enough to supply their need, because it would greatly increase the currency without impairing the relative equivalency of its individual units.

The Republican Party reply to this proposal to change the existing monetary conditions, that such increase of the amount of the currency at this time would greatly reduce the purchasing power of all silver coin, both that already issued and that which might be coined hereafter, and that the risk of such result is so great that this nation should only venture to make such a momentous monetary experiment with the co-operation of the other civilized commercial nations of the world.

The American people are to decide which of these contrasted policies it is better for the greatest nation of the world to pursue. If the claim of those who favor free coinage of silver be true and reliable, that policy is the most beneficent and desirable ever proposed to any government or any people. If it is not, it is one of the most perilous and delusive ever suggested.

Having such immeasurable responsibility resting upon them, it is fit and fortunate that the people are giving to this question such deep, earnest, and universal attention. Instead of deprecating its discussion or visiting those who advocate either view with reprehension or denunciation, it should be regarded as the most hopeful sign of our civilization, the certain evidence that another great step has been taken toward the establishment and perfection of "A government of the people, by the people, and for the people."

Hard words are soft arguments. Passion is a poor guide. The sober thought of an intelligent people can be trusted to decide more wisely than biassed theorists or heated partisans. The destinies of the republic are not decided by the government at Washington, but by free parliaments which gather in the field, the shop, the school-house, and by the fireside. It is only when the people grow apathetic that the Republic is in peril.

Whatever may be the result of this great "Battle of the Standards" now pending, one thing is sure—the world will be better for its being fought out by the "heart, brain, and conscience of the American people," in discharge of the great function of self-government which rests equally with all, rich and poor, high and low.

II.

WHAT IS THE ISSUE?

THE story is told of a noted English judge, that he was wont to assure the jury in all cases of difficulty that when they had once clearly determined what the questions were which they had to decide, their work would be at least half done.

This principle is especially applicable to the duty which at this time devolves on the American people. At first glance the issue seems simplicity itself, but like that of guilty or not guilty, it is found on examination to depend on the prior determination of a great variety of curiously obscure and complicated theories. Yet there is no reason why a man of ordinary capacity should not determine for himself the essential questions and arrive at an intelligent conclusion on the merits of the issue presented.

At first glance one is struck by the apparent simplicity of the proposed policy of free coinage of silver, the ruin which attended its revocation and the dazzling magnificence of the results which are to flow from its restoration. There are not really many facts involved, and there is little, if any, controversy in regard to them. The

times are hard; have been for years. We are a producing
people—the greatest producing people in the world, both
in extent and variety of products. Prices are low—lower
than they have ever been in our country's history. Corn,
wheat, all kinds of cereals ; cattle, horses, cotton, iron,
steel—everything—or almost everything that is raised on
the farm or made in the shop has been marked down and
down until even the purchaser marvels at the cheapness
of what he buys. The wages of labor are not only
greatly reduced, but opportunity for employment is
greatly restricted. Capital is timid ; enterprise is
paralyzed. Even the hope of better times seems to
have little to rest upon. Yet there was never so much
wealth, never so much luxury, never so much capital
lying idle, never so much debt, never so much abundance, yet never so many out of work ; never so much
difficulty to procure ordinary comforts ; never so many
idle men.

All this is true by every one's observation and experience.

What is the cause of these conditions ? This is the
universal, the inevitable inquiry. No man can help
asking it. It is an intuitive expression of wonder inspired by unexpected, if not unparalleled, conditions.
The advocate of free coinage answers promptly : " The
demonetization of silver. " " When did that occur ? "
" In 1873." " Sure enough," the inquirer reflects, " and
there came a big ' panic ' just afterwards, and things
have been going on from bad to worse ever since. But

how," he asks, " did this demonetization of silver come to have such a wonderful effect ? "

The answer comes with fluent confidence : " It reduced the volume of the currency ; increased the purchasing power of gold ; and so lowered the price of everything which is bought and sold."

" How can these conditions be remedied ? " By repealing the " crime of 1873"—by re-monetizing silver, thereby increasing the volume of currency, restoring silver to its " god-ordained use as a coin metal," making money abundant, business lively, prices high, and the demand for labor greater than ever before.

It is a dazzling contrast, and so simple and easy to be effected ! We have only to coin silver night and day, as the world brings it to our mints and the miners dig it out of the ground. There is an amazing store of it waiting to be made into round white plasters which are to bring balm to the world's woes ! One wonders if the prosperity which is promised will be at all proportionate with the superabundance of the remedy. It seems reasonable that it should be, and one can only hope it might. But as to this, no prophet gives assurance. We know there must be an immense amount of the redeeming metal waiting transmutation into coin. There has been little coined in twenty-five years except those 365,000,000 silver dollars which persist in lying idle in the vaults of the Treasury at Washington, instead of flowing forth to heal the nations in spite of " the government stamp " upon them. During this time, the product has averaged

$150,000,000 a year. The mints of Europe have been practically closed for twenty years. With the old stock, which other nations are waiting to let us have,— Germany alone has $400,000,000 of depreciated coin to dispose of—there must be not far from $1,000,000,000 of silver waiting to have its purchasing power expanded one half by the impress of our mint-mark with the boastful legend " In God we trust." Practically, this claim of the advocates of free coinage means that the wealth of the world will be at once increased more than a billion dollars by the simple coinage of what is now in sight. If the theory be a true one, there was never anything like it for beneficent results. But IS it true? There is the rub. And if it be not true, what would the consequences be? There lies the danger.

Because of this doubt, it becomes necessary to consider the nature of money and recall something of its history in order to judge what the probabilities may be that the result promised will be secured.

As has been said, the facts in the case are not many, and most of them are substantially agreed upon. It is only the consequences claimed to result from these facts which are affected with doubt. Let us see in what there is agreement, and then we shall more easily define the doubt. It is agreed that the advocates of free coinage of silver, are right in the following facts on which they base their conclusions :

The silver dollar was the original standard of equivalency in the United States.

Gold was afterwards made a co-ordinate standard of the ratio of sixteen parts of coined silver as equivalent to one of coined gold.

At the time the California gold fields were opened, 1849, silver was worth *more* than this ratio in the market.

The commercial value of silver continued to be above its coin-value in the United States until after 1873.

The annual production of gold during this interval 1849, to 1873, exceeded in value that of silver.

The *commercial* value of silver fell below the *coin*-value in France and most of the continental nations of Europe before 1870 ; the ratio in these countries being one to fifteen and one half ; that is, *less* silver is there—required as a coin-equivalent for gold than with us.

Gold has not fallen in value since 1849 ; it *may* even have appreciated.

The prices of nearly all commodities have fallen since 1873, but there are certain noteworthy exceptions.

The price of commodities had been falling from 1865 to 1873.

The price of most commodities, whether natural products or manufactured articles, is perhaps lower now than at any period in the world's history.

Supply and demand are the *chief* regulators of prices for all commodities. If there is a short supply, prices range high ; if an abundant supply, prices are low.

In 1873 the United States stopped coining silver *on private account.*

Nearly all of the nations of Europe had restricted the

coinage of silver before that time, or had initiated movements looking to its restriction.

With these facts admitted, we have to consider the questions on which the validity of the claims of the advocates of free coinage of silver rest, to wit :

Did the restriction of the coinage of silver on private account *by the United States in 1873* cause the depreciation of silver ?

Did the adoption of the gold dollar of twenty-five and four-fifths grains fine gold as the standard of equivalency by the United States in 1873 cause the depreciation of silver ?

Did the establishment of the gold standard of equivalency, or the repeal of the law permitting coinage of silver on private account by the United States, or both of them, cause the decline in prices since that time ?

Will the free coinage of silver cause silver to appreciate ?

Will the free coinage of silver cause the prices of commodities to rise ?

Does an increase in the currency ever cause a general advance in the price of commodities ?

Is it *possible* that the value of silver and the price of commodities should BOTH be enhanced by free coinage of silver ?

Even granting that the restriction of silver coinage in 1873 was a " crime," is it at all certain that its repeal would be a cure ?

If it should happen that the results of free coinage

should *not* be what its advocates anticipate, but on the contrary should be a debased currency and still further depression in all lines of production and trade, how long will it take the country to recover, and what would be the cost of restoring our currency ?

Cannot our currency be increased to any extent that may be desirable, without any of the risk attending free-coinage, without disturbing the present standard, at a great reduction of the public interest-charge, without any of the present difficulty arising from the use of our credit-currency to draw gold from the treasury, and without modification of the present standard ?

Even if the best currency, abstractly considered, should be gold and silver coined without restriction, at a ratio of sixteen to one, might not occasions arise which would make it ruinous to a country's prosperity, to adopt such a currency, and are not the existing conditions of our currency and our finances such as to constitute the present such an occasion ?

These are questions which every man must answer, before he can intelligently determine which side he will take in the present " battle of the standards." As will be seen, they are mostly questions depending upon present conditions rather than upon historic theories. They are not difficult to answer, if, instead of trying to guess financial conundrums, one will devote his attention to the consideration of well-known facts.

In considering these questions, we shall endeavor to avoid immaterial detail and the discussion of abstract theories, however interesting they may be, unless of absolute importance to the questions in issue, the purpose being to present the subject clearly to every reader whether he be a technical expert in the minor details of monetary theories or not.

III.

AN OLD, OLD STORY.

THE "battle of the standards" is no new thing.
Cæsar took part in one of its skirmishes and Coper-
nicus wrote a book about it before he formulated his
theory of the solar system. Those who wrote about it
until the middle of the eighteenth century were mostly
priests and philosophers. Then the French school of
social writers, with some great financiers of the time,
took it up. Toward the last of that century, Adam
Smith, Ricardo, and other great thinkers, considered it,
generally, as a part of some work on political economy
of which it is a necessary branch. Since 1870, when the
demonetization of silver in the continental nations of
Europe was first considered as a practical question, the
flood of works which have flowed from the presses of
England, Germany, France, and the United States upon
this subject has been enormous. All sorts of people
have written upon it, but especially college professors,
bankers or professional financiers and social and political reformers. A curious thing about it is that very
few lawyers have contributed to the volume of this
literature. Perhaps the reason for this may be found in

the indefinite and conflicting character of speculation upon the subject, as, indeed, upon all branches of what is termed the "science" of political economy. The defects of nearly all the works upon the subject —defects common to all branches of politico-economic speculation—have been : (1) An apparently irresistible inclination to formulate a universal system of monetary philosophy applicable to all times and conditions, nations and peoples. (2) A like tendency, especially on the part of social reformers, to devise monetary systems which shall harmonize with some pet theory and wrest the work of other writers on the subject to support their peculiar views ; the object of most of this class of writers being not to perfect the existing monetary system, but to devise one that may support and strengthen some peculiar social theory.

Except in metaphysical philosophy, there has never been anything like the same amount of theorizing with such a notable paucity of facts. Almost every writer's purpose seems to have been to demolish some other writer's theory. Some of the works have been wonderfully astute studies of particular topics, and the tendency is a growing one in that direction. A very large proportion of them, however, are concerned with the same old problem—how to arrive at and maintain a correct and stable relation between two coin-metals, which arose in the earliest times from the apparent insufficiency in the supply of a single metal to serve as the sole medium of exchange. At that time, credit-money had not been devised, and coin and private credit were the only agencies of exchange. Consequently, neither silver nor gold was deemed sufficient alone to meet the demands of trade. So the battle of the standards began. Reduced to its simplest terms, it is an inquiry as to how two things, each of constantly varying value, can be kept at a stable ratio of equivalency to each other. This problem has occupied the minds of men just about as long as the study of perpetual motion. Like that queer problem of mechanics, it has attracted some of the best minds of every succeeding age, and is to-day just about as near solution.

For several years the writer pursued the study of this subject with undiminished ardor, expecting always to find somewhere set forth a universal science of national finance to which all monetary questions might be referred for final and infallible decision. At the end of that time, he reached the conclusion that such a science is just as impossible of formulation as a universal science of business methods. One man pursues one method and succeeds ; another its opposite and succeeds. One man makes a fortune by operating railroads ; another by wrecking them. The same man pursues one method at one time and succeeds ; the same method at another time and fails. At one time, it is sound policy or a grim necessity for him to pay twenty, fifty, or even a hundred per cent. interest ; at another, he would be a fool to borrow at ten. To-day, it is sound policy for him to buy at the highest rate ; to-morrow equally to his interest to sell at half what property may have cost him. In other words, business methods must depend on the man, the conditions and opportunities he meets, and the character of those with whom he deals.

In like manner, national financial policy and monetary methods must depend on the genius of the people, the financial condition of the nation, the credit and re- sources of that particular country at any special juncture of its affairs. In other words, the monetary system of every nation should be adapted to promote its prosperity.

Thus the monetary methods' of the United States dur- ing the War of the Rebellion were, in many respects, such as to make the hair of the professional financier or money theorist stand up with horror in their contempla- tion. But they were fitted to the genius of the people and the conditions of the times, and were unquestionably the best that could have been devised. They were not, as some have claimed, exceptions to a general rule, but applications of the one sole universal rule : *Monetary methods and financial policies must be adapted to existing conditions.*

Impressed by this view, the author has formulated some brief maxims, which may be found helpful to one studying some of the current literature on this subject :

A preconceived theory is the worst kind of a torch to guide the footsteps of an inquirer after truth.

The fact that a man is a successful banker or great capitalist no more constitutes him a reliable authority as to what constitutes the most desirable currency for a country to adopt at a particular juncture, than skill with the rifle constitutes the marksman an authority on the science of projectiles or the composition of gunpowder.

The reformer who regards currency as merely a means for effecting some ulterior social or economic result, and, therefore, proposes a currency which shall be good enough to pay debts and poor enough to draw the teeth of avarice, may be a very good man, but is not likely to arrive at safe conclusions on practical questions.

Money is an instrument of human invention susceptible of constant improvement but subject to no natural law, except the law of human nature and the limitations of supply and demand.

The improvement of this instrument of trade in the past has been as pronounced as the development of any material art, and has arisen from the stress of public need rather than elaboration of pre-existing theory. Its perfection has been delayed by the conditions which have prevented the application of the inventive faculty to the elaboration of its mechanism.

Sound judgment, applied to a clear comprehension of existing financial conditions, is the only thing that can be safely relied on to solve the present problem. This is quite as apt to be found in the man who walks the furrow as in one who discounts bills.

The force of "authority" in monetary science is greatly impaired by a general tendency to make the Almighty responsible for pet projects. The truth is that God has nothing more to do with money than with bicycles. He furnishes the raw material and the man who makes and uses both—and that is all.

It may not be polite to look a gift-horse in the mouth; but when one makes his fellow-citizens a present of a new political theory, it becomes their duty as trustees for each other's welfare, to examine its teeth before exchanging old methods for it.

The more positive a man's assertions, the more anxious one should be to examine his premises.

A man who proposes to jump over a precipice should be sure there is some way of getting back ; and one who advocates a policy should consider what would be the result if his prognostications chance to fail. A safe and sure remedy should always be preferred to a doubtful and dangerous one.

These may be commonplace truths ; but if one is going to try to find his way through the maze of assertion, theory, assumption, and whimsicality which constitutes the great mass of speculation in regard to "value," "wealth," and the relations of collective power to individual conditions put forth in the present campaign, he will need to strengthen his sense of personal responsibility for the result very often, by recurring to them. There is nothing so contagious as reiterated error. When a specious falsehood is closely tagged to a self-evident truth, it is very hard to separate them. Mohammed understood this fundamental principle of human nature and linked with the universal truth, "God is God," the specious non-sequitur, "and Mahomet is his prophet." In social and economic speculation, a little bit of known truth is often made to float an immense amount of untested theory.

In the following pages the writer has endeavored to confine himself to the discussion of a single question : "What is the best monetary policy for the United States to adopt at this time ? "

IV.

THE WORLD'S VERDICT.

In attempting to answer this question, it is a matter of importance that we keep always in mind the fact that *money is a purely human invention.* Fortunately for the reverence due to him, the Almighty has nothing to do with the form, character, composition, value or efficiency of any kind of money. The utmost that can be said, is that He created the substances to which the function of money has been attached by various human devices. That is, He made the shells which men polished or perforated and used for currency; the materials out of which wampum was woven; the skins which passed current when fairly dressed, the metal which a legal unit-mark transmutes into coin; the raw materials of the paper on which the promise which constitutes credit-money is impressed.

> " God made bees, bees made honey;
> God made man, man made money,"

is an old saw which tells the whole story of the divine relation to both products. The bee's instinct for a saccharine diet impelled him to gather and store honey. Man's inclination to better his condition by trade with his neighbor induced him to devise an instrument to facilitate exchange. The bee having only a limited intelligence contents itself with one sort of cell-formation, and as soon as it finds it unnecessary, by reason of milder climate, to store honey for winter use, he quits work entirely. The more a man gets, however, the more he wants ; and when he finds one form of money cumbersome or insufficient for his needs, he devises another.

It is much the same relation that the migratory impulse in man sustains to the improvement of the means of marine propulsion. A savage struggling to keep afloat in some forgotten flood, seized on a log and was borne down with the current. After a while, he burnt out one side of the log and had a canoe. Another stuck up a leafy branch and made a sail ; another invented a paddle, another an oar. The canoe, in time, became a boat ; the boat a ship. Masts and yards were provided, a rudder was added. After thousands of years the compass came to give eyes to the winged caravel, and the log to measure its speed. After some centuries more, a man harnessed steam to a great cumbrous, unscientific, yet wonder-working side-wheel propeller and bade defiance to wind and tide. Twenty-five years after, so swift had come to be the march of invention, a screw-propeller was tucked under the stern and did the work of the side-wheels much better and with less risk of disablement. Sails, oars, paddles, and side-wheels are still in use, but the screw-propeller is the type of excellence. Who shall say that to-morrow may not show a much better form of marine propeller? It is hardly to be doubted that it will soon come. What would be said of a mariner or philosopher who should clamorously assert that the paddle, the oar, or the sail were the only "natural," "god-ordained," "safe and reliable " means of traversing river and ocean? Simply that they were too crazy to be out of bedlam or too stupid to know what they were talking about.

The improvement in the form and character of money has not been so marked as of the means of marine propulsion, nor has it reached a scientific perfection at all comparable with that of the screw-propeller. Indeed, it may be doubted if it has reached a stage of efficiency equivalent to that of the side-wheeler in marine architecture. There are good and sufficient reasons for this slowness of development and imperfection of results. A monetary system can only be improved through the action of a sovereign power, and the sovereign, whether individual or popular, is always hard to move forward. The marine architect needs no legislative permit to try his experiments ; the man who seeks to improve the instrument of exchange must convince a king or a country that what has been is not perfection, and that what he suggests is an improvement. Collective progress is always away behind individual development. Our governments, state and national, were urged to take control of the telegraph. For a mere trifle, fifty years ago, the nation might have secured those inventions which are the foundation of the great telegraph monopoly of to-day. Now the wires are stronger than the government, and it is likely to require as many more years to enable it to break the coil of the python which sucks the blood of the people. Governments move slowly because individuals have to go ahead and drag them forward. It is for this reason that improvements in the monetary system of a country are never made except from stress of public loss or disaffection. When a monetary idea has been quite worn out, or a king or country is in such straits that something must be done, the statesman turns his attention for a time to improving the currency. The ratchet is loosed a cog or two, and then locked up until another " monetary crisis " kicks it loose again. Honest coin of uniform weight and standard fineness, credit-money, bank-bills, legal-tender promises,—these and other improvements in the instrument of exchange which we call money, are all the result of popular disaffection with existing monetary conditions.

Another reason why progress in this direction has been slow, is the fact that until recent times, the monarch and the money-lender were the persons whose interest was chiefly considered in all matters affecting the money of the realm. The monarch debased the currency at his need, or paid the money-lender in concessions of privilege, which enabled him not only to recoup his loan, but secured to him profits which the people had to pay. To this we are indebted for many of the most vicious principles of finance, among others the theory of constant redeemability as the sole basis of credit-currency.

Still another reason, which should by no means be overlooked, is the inherent conservatism of wealth. Not only the large capitalist, but the man of moderate means looks with a just and reasonable suspicion upon changes in the circulating medium. Mere unfounded apprehension of change sometimes crystallizes into invincible opposition, and there are instances in monetary history, in which attempts tò introduce a better currency have been baffled by this sentiment. There is no doubt that much of the popular revulsion against the gold standard in 1878 was based on this feeling, rather than any special conviction that the "dollar of the fathers" would give us a better currency. The same sentiment showed itself in continental Europe, and was reflected in the monetary congresses of the next few years.

Despite these influences, experiments intended to increase the volume of the currency have been not infrequent in civilized countries. The great majority of them have been more or less successful attempts to use banking-credit regulated by law, to supplement some coinage system, the object being in almost every case both to increase the circulating medium and enable the bank to make a profit by the fiction of issues constantly redeemable in coin. The record of the failures, panics, and disasters which have resulted should be sufficient to convince any one of the folly, if not the wickedness, of this inherently absurd theory, and should long ago have compelled its abandonment and the substitution of some more philosophical and less perilous method of supplementing a nation's coinage. It seems to have a peculiar charm, however, for the speculative intellect and the most noted writers on financial questions still insist that a method depending wholly on chance and the skill of the banker is the only secure foundation for a credit-currency.

Of the other experiments which have been made by the nations of the world, having for their purpose the improvement of credit-currency, there are but three that are worthy of note at this time : (1) The grant of legal-tender quality to the notes of the Bank of England, the Bank of France, and other national European banks ; (2) The issue of non-interest bearing legal-tender demand-notes by the government of the United States in 1862 and their maintenance as an important part of the currency until the present time. (3) The establishment of our system of National Banks, whose issues are based entirely on the credit of the government, represented by bonds deposited to secure circulation and redeemable in legal money of the United States.

These are important and instructive steps towards the improvement of credit-currency as an adjunct of the coinage systems of these countries.

As to the experiments in coinage, it may be said broadly, that every country of the world has at some time in its history taken a turn at the problem of discovering the proper ratio of equivalency between gold and silver, and then trying to keep such ratio stable. All of these experiments may be classed under the following heads :

1.—The attempt to maintain a stable equivalency by the use of both gold and silver as coin metals of equal dignity and unrestricted coinage at some fixed ratio of equivalency. This experiment may be said to have been tried by every nation of the world and been abandoned as hopeless by nearly all, practically, by all. England abandoned it in 1816 ; France, Italy, Switzerland, Greece, Belgium, Austria, Germany, the United States, Portugal, Brazil, Chili, Egypt, Norway, Sweden, Denmark, during the past quarter of a century, that is, at various times since 1870.

2.—The countries named above having abandoned unrestricted coinage of *both* metals at a fixed ratio of equivalency, have entered upon the experiment of an unlimited coinage of gold, which is made the standard of equivalency, with a *restricted* coinage of silver at a fixed ratio of equivalency, not uniform in all of them, being sixteen to one in the United States, fifteen and a half to one in most of the others and fourteen and one-fourth to one in Great Britain. This experiment differs in one important respect, in different countries. In the United States, France, and most of the continental countries in Europe, except Germany, the experiment is being tried, of a *restricted* silver coinage being maintained, with full legal-tender power ; that is, making it a legal-tender for all debts, no matter what their amount.

In England, Germany, and perhaps Austria, the experiment is being tried of limiting the legal-tender power of the *restricted* silver coinage, that is, making silver coin

a legal-tender only for limited amounts ; in England the
limit is forty shillings. For any less amount, silver is
a legal-tender. This has been the English monetary
system, substantially, since 1816. In other words, she
has tried this experimeut for eighty years.

3.—In all the countries above named with an infinite
variety of difference in method, the coinage has been
supplemented by some system of legal-tender credit-
money, issued either by the government directly, or by
some banking institution, to which the privilege has been
granted as a profitable concession.

4.—In all of them the experiment has been tried, of
keeping their legal-tender credit-money at par with the
standard equivalency by the application of the monetary
theory of " constant redeemability " ; that is, the legal-
tender credit-money is said to be at all times redeemable
in coin of full legal-tender quality.

5.—Certain other countries which have also abandoned
the experiment of unrestricted coinage of two metals
of equal dignity, at a fixed ratio, have attempted to solve
the problem of the stability of coin-equivalency, by
abandoning gold as a coin-metal, that is, by demonetizing gold and retaining silver as the only legal-tender
coin. These countries are Mexico, British India, Central America, Bolivia, Columbia, Ecuador, Peru, and
Venezuela. Russia is preparing to adopt the gold standard. Japan and China are, practically, on a silver basis.

6.—Certain other countries are still continuing the experiment of a double or bi-metallic standard of equiva-

lency. These are: The Argentine Republic, Hayti, The Netherlands, Spain, Servia, and Turkey. These are termed experiments, because all things are experimental which are subject to change or modification. They are all attempts made by various nations to determine the monetary system best adapted to the peculiar conditions of each, and are entitled to consideration and respect as such. Their value, as analogies or arguments, in the pending controversy in the United States, is to be estimated by our knowledge of the social, financial, and economic conditions of each of these nations. Fortunately, every person of ordinary intelligence is able to apply this test with more or less accuracy and determine for himself which is more likely to afford a safe example for us to follow at this time, and it needs but a single glance at the lists above given to show that every nation of any commercial or political importance in the world has abandoned after fair and prolonged trial the attempt to maintain a stable equivalency by the unrestricted coinage of two precious metals. The more intelligent and prosperous have adopted the single gold standard with a restricted silver coinage. The class of nations next in consequence have adopted silver as the standard of equivalency, either wholly demonetizing gold or forcing it into the condition of a commodity. There are still some men of very high intellectual character who insist on what is termed the double or bi-metallic standard as both practical and desirable, just as there are still men who believe in perpetual motion.

3

So far as national experience goes, however, it has decided overwhelmingly in favor of a mono-metallic standard of equivalency.

The advocates of the unrestricted coinage of silver seek to break the force of this world-verdict against their theory, by asserting that the other nations of the world have been forced to this position by the predominating power of British capital. The claim, if worth considering at all, is greatly weakened by the fact that the three nations most hostile to British interests and most jealous of British influences, France, Germany, and the United States, have only given over the double standard theory during the past twenty-five years. The writer confesses himself an Anglophobist of the rankest sort, but he sees no reason for running counter to all the world's experience, simply because some one chooses to point to the result and say: "See what England has done!" The fact that England has adhered to the gold standard for so many years is simply the testimony of the nation which has the most successfully and persistently nourished and developed her commercial interests. In the matter of free-trade, there are evident reasons why her example should not be followed. In the matter of the standard of equivalency no such reasons have yet been assigned. The idea of injuring her financially, by demonetizing gold and compelling our people to buy it at a premium to pay ten or more billion dollars of existing gold-debts, is too evident an absurdity to need rebuttal.

Practically, we may say that the whole world has decided against the unrestricted coinage of two metals. All the great commercial nations of Europe and America have adopted the gold-standard ; the most part of them after a long struggle. All the great nations of Asia, with Mexico and Central America, have also decided against the double-standard and adopted silver. What should be the force of this verdict ?

It is not to be denied that the world may be wrong in this matter ; but it lies with those who claim that it is, to prove the fact beyond a reasonable doubt before they ask the people of the United States to accept their theory.

Under the circumstances, it becomes important to consider whether we would better seek to cure our financial ills by making another attempt to solve the old riddle in the old way, or try to find a remedy at least not inconsistent with the world's experience. Shall we go back to the canoe, or improve the side-wheeler ?

V.

MONETARY EXPERIMENTS.

OUR own financial history has been very prolific in experiments intended to improve or increase the currency. Most of these have been along the line of bank-issues of substitute-money, being almost infinitely varied devices for making more or less cash plus a great deal of credit sustain the fiction of the constant redeemability of such issues. Some of these experiments were quite remarkable for the ingenuity displayed in making nothing seem to be equivalent to something. They very properly earned for our State-bank issues the name of "wild-cat currency," by the amazing agility displayed in ascending and descending the scale of equivalency, it being absolutely necessary that a business man should carry a bank-note directory in order to keep track of the shrinkage from day to day of various issues of substitute-money.

To this experience with state banks of issue, has been added that of a great national institution, the fiscal agent of the government controlling its funds and having the use of its deposits. Its overthrow constitutes one of the most dramatic episodes of our history. The suf-

36

fering that resulted is even yet one of the most vivid remembrances of the elders of to-day who were the children or youths of that epoch.

This experience has been supplemented by two of the most remarkable experiments in the field of credit-money ever made, to wit : 1. The issue by the government of demand-notes professing constant redeemability in coin, at a time when such redeemability was known to be impossible ; their maintenance without any pretense of fulfilment of this pledge, as an important and fairly stable part of the currency for seventeen years ; the ultimate redemption of this long-deferred promise by the resumption of specie-payments in 1879 ; the evils that resulted from the constant redeemability of these demand-liabilities, after they had served the purposes of currency with admirable stability and convenience for thirty years, when the attempt to preserve a parity of value between even a restricted silver currency and gold caused a " run " upon the treasury for gold which there was no legal method of supplying except by increase of the bonded debt.

This experiment, extending over thirty-four years, the most momentous in the monetary and financial history of the world, is unquestionably the most important ever made in the field of credit-money. Its long-continued efficiency and close approach to permanent success, must suggest to the dullest comprehension the belief that its defects are certainly remediable. As a matter of fact, its partial failure during recent years was wholly due to the abandonment of one of the fundamental principles on which it was based—to wit, the payment of customs duties in gold in order to provide a continuous supply of gold coin to meet the constant redeemability of these issues. Left without this safeguard by the clamorous but wholly illogical demand that the nation should receive its promises to pay in discharge of *all* obligations to itself, the treasury was exposed to a continuous demand for gold without any authorized means of obtaining it except making loans to secure a constantly threatened reserve. This was aggravated if not precipitated by the strenuous and heroic efforts of the government to maintain a parity of equivalency between our silver coinage supplemented by more than half a billion dollars of silver-certificates, and gold. Nothing so clearly shows the amazing strength of our national credit as the fact that, despite this unequal and hopeless struggle, our terminal-credit or bonded debt has remained at a premium unequalled in the history of national finance.

2. Another remarkable experiment in the field of credit-money was the establishment of our present system of National Banks. The features which distinguish this from all other systems of banks of issue are : (1) That its issues are wholly secured by the deposit of terminal-credit or interest-bearing bonds of the country. (2) That the government guarantees the payment of its issues and regulates their amount, and (3) that its issues are redeemable not in coin, but in any lawful money of the United States. The credit of these issues rests

entirely upon the public confidence in this guarantee, not being affected in the slightest degree by the stability or financial condition or repute of the bank in whose name they are issued. It presents, therefore, the unprecedented anomaly of a banking system the stability of whose issues is unaffected by the failure of the bank which puts them in circulation. The notes of a "broken" National bank pass current just as readily as those of the most stable and prosperous. Only one objection obtains to this remarkable experiment—the cost of the currency thus provided. This cost consists of two elements—the interest on the bonds deposited to secure the issues and the exemption of both bonds and issues from state and municipal taxation. The former element alone makes the cost of $250,000,000 of these issues based on four per cent. bonds $10,000,000 a year. The amount of the other element of cost, exemption from taxation, is not easily determinable.

3. A third notable experiment was the issue of silver-certificates, a consequence of the policy of upholding to the utmost limit of the national credit, the parity of equivalency between silver and gold at the ratio of 16 to 1. These certificates pledge the government to pay to the bearer on demand the number of silver dollars mentioned in each. Being exchanged, in the course of business, for legal-tender treasury-notes which are redeemable in coin, they become, indirectly, redeemable in gold. They represent the larger part of our silver coinage in circulation. By this system of continuous ex-

change it results, therefore, that the demand for gold which has recently caused so large an increase of our bonded debt, is in reality only a constantly recurring redemption of our silver coinage or its equivalent, silver-certificates, in gold coin. This experiment is valuable as showing that there is a limit to the ability of even the richest and most prosperous nation of the world to maintain with its credit, parity of value between two constantly diverging standards of equivalency. It also proves the practicability of making the terminal-credit of the nation the basis of a phenomenally stable and uniform credit-currency.

Without further consideration of details, it may be said that our monetary experiments thus far, have established beyond question the following propositions :

I. A great national bank, modelled on the plan of the great banking institutions of Europe, whether it be the fiscal agent of the government or not, is an aggregation of monetary power obnoxious to the genius of our people.

II. That a system of state banks, controlled by the several commonwealths of the Union, lacks stability and uniformity to a degree altogether unlikely ever again to command popular approval.

III. That the demand-notes of the government were a thoroughly satisfactory and stable currency until they came to be used by the traffickers in currency as a convenient means for collecting gold for speculative purposes.

IV. That the *terminal*-credit of the United States, that is, its bonds, is kept above par without difficulty and for almost any conceivable amount.

V. That the present system of National Banks, the issues of which are redeemable, not in coin, but in any "legal money of the United States," has been the most stable, uniform, and equable bank-currency ever known, *because* its issues are sustained by the amazing desirability of the *terminal*-credit—that is, the interest-bearing bonds of the United States.

These results necessarily suggest the inquiry whether it is not better to seek a remedy for our present monetary evils in some other direction than by continuing the attempt to secure the stable equivalency of even a restricted coinage of two precious metals at a fixed ratio.

VI.

" THE CRIME (?) OF 1873."

THE only coinage experiment of any importance which has been made thus far in the monetary history of the United States consists of four remarkable acts—that of 1873, now held up to popular condemnation by the advocates of the unrestricted coinage of silver as "the crime of '73," the act of 1878, which was the result of popular protest against the restriction of silver-coinage, the modification of the latter by the act of 1890, and the repeal of the purchasing clause of this latter act, popularly known as the "Sherman Bill," in 1893. To these may be added the various measures adopted during this interval intended to stimulate the use and circulation of silver coins and their equivalents, silver-certificates. Among these may be mentioned the prohibition of further issues of national-bank notes and greenbacks under the denomination of five dollars, and the authorization of silver-certificates of the denominations of one and two dollars. This legislation, extending over a period of eighteen years, supplemented as it has been by almost incredible exertions of successive secretaries of the Treasury to give it effect, is well entitled to rank as the most stupendous experiment ever made in the long-continued battle of the standards having for its object the maintenance of parity of equivalency between two coin-metals. Its details are so numerous as to be confusing to one who attempts to master the relations of each to the real issue involved. Advantage has been taken of this complexity to give an altogether false impression of the real purpose and character of these acts. The story in detail from 1879 until 1890, is given with wonderful accuracy and fulness in Prof. Taussig's remarkable brochure, *The Silver Situation in the United States* (G. P. Putnam's Sons, New York). Unfortunately this work, like many others of similar character, while leaving nothing to be desired in its treatment of the subject within specified limits, has failed to impress upon the popular mind the true relation of these acts to the question that underlies the conflict between silver and gold, by showing that the very purposes avowed by the advocates of "free silver" may more easily and surely be attained by other means. Instead of advocating the amendment of our credit-currency as a means both of remedying the evils of our monetary system and reducing the interest-charge of our public debt, they advocate its retirement and a consequent increase of bond indebtedness.

What, in brief, were the provisions of these acts and their true relation to our monetary and financial conditions? The act of 1873, designated by the advocates of unrestricted silver coinage as a "crime of inconceivable enormity," so far as the character of the currency is concerned, consisted of two provisions, to wit: (1) It made the gold dollar of 25⅘ grains of fine gold the standard of equivalency. (2) It prohibited the further coinage of silver *on private account.* It did not demonetize silver already coined, but left it a full legal-tender at the existing ratio of sixteen to one.

The act of 1878, also, consisted of two relevant provisions : (1) It required the government to purchase every month two million dollars' worth of silver bullion for coinage into silver dollars. This, at the market value at that time, amounted very nearly to the total silver production of the United States. (2) It provided for the issue of silver-certificates, each entitling the holder to a specified number of silver dollars on demand.

The act of 1890 required the Secretary of the Treasury to purchase each month four and a half million ounces of silver bullion at the market price, and pay for it in treasury-notes of the United States, which it made full legal-tender for the payment of all debts. It also made them redeemable in either gold or silver coin at the discretion of the Secretary of the Treasury, and required every possible effort to be made to keep silver at a parity of equivalency with gold. This provision was especially emphatic and was accompanied by a provision that the treasury-notes authorized by it might be issued in denominations as low as one dollar, in order that silver might take the place of the greenbacks and

national-bank notes of denominations less than five dollars which were withdrawn from circulation by the act
of 1885.

Was the act of 1873 a crime? What are the reasons
given for denouncing it as such? It is claimed that it
caused the depreciation of silver ; that by restricting
the currency, it caused the general decline in prices
which has since occurred ; that it was inspired by capitalists, bankers, the Rothschilds, " gold-bugs," and various other demoniac influences, whose purpose was to
oppress the poor and consume the debtor ; that silver
being " the poor man's money," the adoption of the gold
standard of equivalency tends to make the rich richer
and the poor poorer. All these allegations, except the
motive alleged, are said to be proved by the tendencies
and conditions developed in the United States since that
time.

So far as the motive is concerned, it is a reflection on
every American citizen to assume that any considerable
body of our people desire to oppress the weak or im-
poverish the poor. Parties and peoples are always sincere. They may make mistakes, but they never commit
crimes. The slave-holder just as firmly believed slavery
to be promotive of the general welfare as its opponents
believed it subversive of justice.

What were the circumstances under which this
act, charged to have been inspired by unholy
purposes and attended with such malign consequences, was adopted? The credit of the United

States had been just as important an element of its success in putting down the rebellion and preserving the
union as the patriotism of our people. It armed the
soldier and fed him while he fought. Because of this,
every utterance of the government and the universal
voice of the people, day after day, through the long years
of conflict, was a continuing pledge to all the world that
we would pay every obligation, keep the national honor
untarnished, and make our currency equal to the best.
For twelve years we had been bravely striving to redeem
this pledge.   For twelve years specie payments had been
suspended. We were struggling on toward resumption
under a load of debt, a very large portion of which,
almost a billion dollars, must soon be refunded. The
great commercial nations of the world to whom we
looked to take our bonds, had adopted the gold standard
or were marching steadily towards it. Silver had already
fallen in value below the ratio in all European countries,
though yet a trifle above our own. The production of
both gold and silver was increasing at a rate unprecedented in the world's history. France, Belgium, Italy,
and Switzerland had just restricted the coinage of silver
by the terms of a common treaty. Germany was struggling to dispose of her vast accumulation of silver and
modelling her monetary system on that which England
had maintained for two hundred years. Could we hope
to resume specie payments in silver ? Who would take
our bonds unless payable, principal and interest, in gold ?
Were we to invite the scorn of the world by repudiating

our obligations as had been done with our " continental currency?" Were we to ask those who had trusted us at home and abroad to take a currency already stricken with blight, which the most intelligent and prosperous nations of the world had rejected or restricted? The supreme duty of the hour was to maintain our credit. It could be done only by the adoption of the gold standard. Even this would have been ineffective had we continued to coin silver *on private account*, to allow every one who had silver bullion to put on it our stamp of equivalency at a ratio greater than its commercial value.

The act of 1873 was neither a crime nor a mistake, but an act of the highest patriotism and the soundest policy. As a result of it, we safely reached the haven of resumption six years later, after seventeen years of suspension, funded our enormous debt, which two years later began to grow steadily less, and in 1879 entered upon the most stupendous struggle to rehabilitate silver in order to benefit our silver producers and encourage and stimulate the development of this industry, that the world has ever witnessed.

Every step in our financial history since 1879 has been intended to promote the use and uphold the parity of equivalency of our silver coinage. Instead of being dominated by " gold-bugs," both of the great parties have been subservient to silver to a degree which has seriously threatened the nation's credit, and has been one of the chief causes of the existing depressed financial conditions.

Silver is, in one sense, it is true, " the poor man's money " :
it is the money of those nations in which the largest
proportion of the most abject and degrading poverty is
found. Look at the list of countries in which silver is
the standard—China, Japan, India, Mexico, Central
America, the Argentine Republic ! It would be unfair to
say that silver has caused the industrial conditions which
there prevail, just as fallacious, indeed, as it is to attribute
our present industrial depression to the act of 1873. This
thing is certain, however : a silver currency has never
shown any tendency toward improving these conditions
—where it has been longest used poverty is most abundant and most blighting in its character. Is it worth
while to intensify poverty in order to secure the adoption of " the poor man's money " ?

VII.

DEPRECIATION OF SILVER.

FINANCIAL and industrial conditions are rarely the result of a single cause or the immediate consequence of a mistaken monetary policy. Indeed, it may perhaps be safely said that except in case of war, famine, pestilence, or other widespread devastating influence, the causes of business depression are never single or immediate. Financially, as well as socially and politically, general conditions are the result of evolutionary influences which develop slowly and become manifest only in results which are apt to be considered causal because of proximity or contemporaneousness, rather than from inherent character and actual potency. One of the most difficult questions presented by the pending controversy in regard to our monetary policy is as to the cause of the depreciation of silver since 1873 and the present general decline of prices. It is perfectly natural, at the first blush, to attribute the former to the adoption of the gold standard, because that was very nearly contemporaneous with the first evidence of marked decline. It is equally natural to attribute the present decline in prices and universal business depression to this change in our

4

monetary system, because of the general impression that money in some mysterious way controls prices and regulates the volume of business.

It is, of course, evident to all that the universal law of supply and demand is an agency of supreme potentiality in determining the rise and fall, within certain limits, of the prices of all commodities. The scarcity of anything which possesses appreciable desirability enhances its value, while its abundance not only reduces its price, but up to a certain point enhances the demand by increasing its use or consumption. So far as the necessaries of life are concerned, the limit of increased demand is reached when all can obtain enough to supply their reasonable needs at existing rates. For instance, the present consumption of breadstuffs cannot be materially increased by any depreciation of prices. No considerable portion of the population of the world would consume any more flour at one dollar a barrel than at the present rate. Even at fifty cents a barrel there would be no generally increased demand, except as men might be tempted to lay in a store for future use. Very few would consume any more than they now do, even if it were obtainable at ten cents a barrel. The limit of consumption is the limit of demand.

In seeking to apply this principle to the depreciation of silver, we are met with certain plausible and, at first sight, apparently insuperable objections. We are told (1) That the chief use of silver being as a coin-metal, the prohibition of its coinage on private account was an interference with the right of the citizen to seek a market for his wares, that is of silver bullion, in their most desirable form ; (2) that such interference with the right of the producer was an artificial restriction of a natural demand which produced an artificial depreciation in its value. (3) That the limit of demand had evidently not been reached, because gold, which is chiefly used for the same purpose, has increased in amount during the past fifty years at an even greater proportional rate than silver, but has not only not depreciated but has, perhaps, even increased in value.

As to the first two of these objections it must be borne in mind that the original demand for silver as a coin-metal was just as artificial as the restriction complained of. Nations chose to adopt silver and gold as coin-metals. They had a perfect right to have adopted any other metals for this purpose, or even to have elaborated a system of currency not based on metallic values at all. But they did adopt these by general accord, and endeavored to fix the ratio of equivalency between them. This varied greatly with the varying supply of each and a variable demand for one or the other. In Cæsar's time it was thought that eight parts of silver were equal in value to one of gold ; then it fell to ten, twelve, fifteen, until, finally, the ratio was fixed in our currency at sixteen to one. This ratio was below the real value of silver—that is, our silver coin was worth more *as silver* than as coin. It was more profitable to buy silver coin to melt than to buy silver bullion to coin. Under these

circumstances, our mints were open to all owners of
bullion to have it coined if they chose. Most of the
continental nations of Europe had fixed the ratio at
fifteen and a half parts of silver to one of gold. Even
at this rate, silver bullion was usually worth more than
gold in the markets of the world. England having fixed
her coin-ratio at about fourteen and a quarter to one,
her silver coinage was depleted by being bought up for
gold, the silver being exported for profit. As a result of
this gold became superabundant, and there was a lack of
silver for the smaller transactions of life. To prevent this,
silver was practically demonetized, that is, its legal-tender
quality was restricted to forty shillings. This prevented
its use in all great monetary transactions, beyond that
amount, and the coinage being restricted and no credit
money under the value of five dollars being allowed, a special field for silver coin was created which at this time requires in coinage $115,000,000 of silver, an amount about
one-fifth as large as its stock of gold, $580,000,000, and
a little larger than the volume of its authorized credit
currency, which is $113,000,000. This policy was sup-
plemented by severe penalties against melting or
exporting silver coin ; the purpose being to keep a
highly appreciated but restricted silver coinage in circulation for small transactions, and to avoid the necessity
and danger of variability of equivalency in its currency. In this manner, as much by accident as by
design, England came to adopt the gold standard of
equivalency.

The United States, having fixed the ratio of equivalency much nearer the commercial value of silver and below that of other countries, that is, requiring more parts of silver to equal one of gold, naturally invited the importation of foreign silver for recoinage here. Besides this, the advantage resulting from the possession of coin in a country but scantily provided with legal-tender and flooded with fluctuating issues of substitute-money was sufficient to overcome any slight variance in value.

Up to 1849, when the mines of California became a distinct factor of the world's supply of precious metals, there was an evident lack of enough coin-metal to supply the demand for legal-tender. This fact was recognized by Great Britain a dozen years before in making the issues of the Bank of England a legal-tender for all debts, and her example was followed a few years later by the government of France, in attaching to the issues of the Bank of France a like legal-tender quality. Both have been continued to this time, and it is to be noted that a large proportion of the issues of both these institutions are based on investments in the national credit of these countries, and the right to issue such legal-tender notes has since been greatly enlarged, especially in France, where the Bank has a monopoly of the issue of credit currency. This expansion of the volume of currency by the issue of authorized legal-tender credit money by two leading commercial nations of the world has been strangely overlooked as an element of the monetary problems which have since arisen, especially in this country.

The entire world-production of gold and silver from 1492 until 1849, is estimated to have amounted to $9,397-,000,000 in value. Of this, $6,413,651,000 was silver and $2,985,437,000 was gold. The production of each of the two metals in 1849 was almost equal in value to the other, being $37,000,000 of gold, and $39,000,000 of silver.

From 1849 until 1872 the production of gold greatly exceeded that of silver, the former being $2,665,000,000 and the latter $1,107,000,000. The aggregate, however, was $3,772,000,000, or more than one-third the entire aggregate production of the previous 350 years. From 1873 until 1894, the production of gold was about equal with that of silver in value, being $2,526,000,000 of gold, and $2,748,000,000 of silver. The aggregate for these twenty-one years amounted, however, to the enormous sum of $5,274,000,000, or more than half the entire world-product from 1492 to 1849! Thus we see that the aggregate increase of coin-metal, including both gold and silver, from 1849 to 1894, amounted to $9,046,000,000, almost equalling the entire production of the world during all the previous period. The production of gold during 1895 and 1896 it is estimated in round numbers will amount to more than $400,000,000 a year, or $800,-000,000 in all. So that we witness the amazing spectacle of the supply of coin-metals having more than doubled in forty-seven years, during which the population of the world cannot have increased over twenty per cent.

Such an enormous increase of coin-metal must of necessity cause some depreciation in its value. This would be expected. But we are met with the startling fact that, in this interval, gold has increased *two and one-half times* the amount produced in the previous three centuries and a half, while silver has only increased about *fifty per cent.* of its previous volume. Yet silver has depreciated in *purchasing power or in commercial value almost one-half, while gold has not depreciated at all!* Why is this? This question we shall answer in the next chapter.

VIII.

A NEW ECONOMIC LAW.

THE law of supply and demand is supposed to be universal : scarcity appreciates and abundance depreciates all values. Hitherto there has been no exception to its operation, save the limitation already pointed out. Yet here is an instance in which the supply of one of the most notable products of the world increases two and one-half times in volume within fifty years and does not depreciate at all, while another product, used for the same purpose, increases only one-half its volume during the same period and depreciates one-half in value. What has caused this difference ?

The answer of the advocates of unrestricted coinage is that the demonetization of silver, that is, the adoption of the gold standard and refusal to coin on private account, has restricted its use and caused its depreciation. Unfortunately for this explanation, it assumes the very fact in question. The real inquiry is what caused the demonetization. The free-silver writers declare it to have been a "gold-bug" conspiracy to appreciate the value of gold. It is said, in reply to this, that the demonetization of silver was a natural result of well-grounded apprehension of the decline which followed. Is this a reasonable hypothesis? Let us see. In 1867, the commercial value of silver fell below 15½ to 1, being 15.57. This had increased in 1873 to 15.92. In 1874 it fell to 16.17, falling below our ratio of 16 to 1 for the first time since its adoption. In 1875 it fell to 16.59, and in 1876 it fell to 17.88. From that time on until 1895, a period of nineteen years, its average yearly decline has been 1.31, falling in that year down to 31.60 to 1.

It will be noted that the depreciation did not become very serious until 1876, and that from 1878 until the present time it has exceeded 1.30 a year. Now it happens as a noteworthy fact, that the combined production of gold and silver during the year 1878, for the first time in the world's history, amounted to more than two hundred million dollars—$214,000,000, in fact—and this has steadily increased until in 1894 it reached the enormous total $397,000,000, and is now more than $400,000,000 a year, with evident prospect of still further increase.

The pertinency of these figures will appear when we consider the fact shown by the report of the Director of the Mint for 1894, that the average coinage of silver during this period amounted, including recoinage, to 92.25 per cent. of the whole annual production of the white metal. So that we have the fact clearly shown that the stock of silver *actually in use* during this period as currency has averaged 92.25 per cent. of the yearly product. In 1873, the aggregate silver currency amounted to

157.34 per cent. of that year's product, while in 1894 it amounted only to 43.76 per cent., a loss of 113.58 per cent. During the same time, the coinage of gold has also fallen off. In 1873 it amounted to 238.31 of the year's supply; in 1894 to 113.53, being a loss of 124.78 per cent. of the year's production. During the whole period, the average amount of gold coin amounted to 106.47 per cent. of the annual gold supply. Can any one believe that the restriction of coinage alone caused a decline in value of silver of 47 per cent., or that mere mintage of the whole surplus and future product would restore it to parity with gold? If it declined *because* it was not minted, why did not gold decline, the coinage of which shrunk during the same period 124.78 per cent. of its annual product, while the coinage of silver only fell off 113.58 per cent. of its yearly product?

The simple fact is, that a higher law than that of any nation has wrought the depreciation of silver—a law whose operation is universal and which the mint-mark of no realm can seriously affect. If all the silver in the world were given the stamp of our coinage to-morrow, the relative value of silver and gold would not be appreciably affected. Why not? Because it is controlled by that immutable law of supply and demand which is a part of universal human nature and controls the ratios that prevail between all appreciable values.

But if the law of supply and demand prevails to control the ratio of value between gold and silver in spite of the ratio of equivalency established by law between coined gold and coined silver, why has not gold depreciated, the supply of which has increased proportionately three times as fast as that of silver?

It is just here that a principle applies which governs the operation of the law of supply and demand in all similar cases. This principle has been entirely neglected in the pending controversy, and, so far as the writer is aware, has never before been clearly formulated. It is as follows :

WHEN TWO MATERIALS, ONE MORE DESIRABLE AND THE OTHER LESS DESIRABLE FOR A PARTICULAR USE, ARE CHIEFLV DEVOTED TO THE SAME GENERAL PURPOSE, AN INCREASED SUPPLY OF ONE OR BOTH TENDS TO THE DEPRECIATION OF THE LESS DESIRABLE, AND DOES NOT SERIOUSLY AFFECT THE MORE DESIRABLE UNTIL THE SUPPLY OF THE LATTER BECOMES SO ABUNDANT AS TO PRACTICALLY SUBSERVE THE ENTIRE USE TO WHICH BOTH WERE ORIGINALLY APPLIED.

In this case, gold and silver were both chiefly used as coin-metals. Gold was preferable to silver, especially in the more important functions of coin, such as redemption reserves and the liquidation of trade balances, because it represents greater value with less bulk and weight. A hundred pounds of it is equal in value to sixteen hundred pounds of silver, so that the mere difference in the cost of transportation gives it immense odds in preferability. Every pound of gold added to the world's stock of coin-metal, therefore, served to reduce not the value of gold, but the value of *coin-metal*, and this loss fell on silver, as the least desirable element of the aggregate supply. When, therefore, the world's supply was doubled, the entire depreciation fell on silver, while gold has maintained its value without perceptible declension.

The *coinage* of gold has declined because it has been found to be even better adapted to the use to which it is chiefly applied, to wit, the liquidation of aggregate balances, in the form of bullion than when coined. It is also more easily estimated and transported with less risk and less waste than when coined. In fact, gold has become chiefly a commodity, the function of which is not to circulate as coin but to liquidate balances with the utmost nicety. While in its coined state it is a legal-tender, the government whose mint-mark it bears never receives it as coin for its face-value, but estimates its value by weight. One may easily prove this by taking an eagle to the Sub-treasury and watching the clerk while he has it weighed to ascertain its real value and estimate how much is required to make it equal to the equivalency represented by its mint-mark.

The same principle is illustrated in the recent fall of horse-values. There was probably an over-production of horses, just as there has been an over-production of silver. But in addition to that, there came also an immense supply of other agencies designed to perform certain of what had been the chief functions of the horse more efficiently than the horse could. The cable and electric cars drove the horse-cars from the streets.

The bicycle superseded the horse in other uses, to which it was especially adapted. Horse-values, as a result, fell to nothing. Why? Because when two things one more and the other less desirable, are devoted to the same specific use, an increase in the supply of either or both, depreciates the less desirable. Bicycles and electric motors are still booming : the horse is rapidly passing from use and has fallen very near to zero in value. Instances of the operation of this law might be multiplied almost indefinitely. An example familiar to all is found in the history of illuminants. Kerosene restricted the demand for animal fats for that purpose. Gas superseded the use of kerosene. Electricity came to take the place of gas. All are yet in use, but the demand for the less desirable illuminants has successively been restricted by the more desirable. Each caused depreciation of the less desirable illuminating agency.

No law can create or long counteract such a tendency. Silver would have depreciated if every ounce which was mined had been coined ; and its depreciation would have been much more rapid but for the heroic action of our government in putting its amazing credit under the galling mass of coin-values. If the production of gold should greatly decrease, the value of silver would probably increase because necessity would compel its use in some form as a currency-basis ; but its desirability cannot be restored by coinage or legislation. Every nation can use a large amount as currency under proper restrictions. A combination of nations might provide for a much larger use ; but no nation or union of nations can hold two unrestricted coinages of varying desirability at a stable ratio of equivalency. The result is inevitable : either there must be a gold-standard with a restricted silver-coinage, or free silver-coinage with gold demonetized or devoted to specific functions. In any case, coinage is certain to be more and more largely supplemented in the future by legal-tender credit money, which has the great advantage of not being liable to any variation with the standard of equivalency, as long as the credit on which it is based is esteemed reliable. The depreciation of silver was an inevitable result of the immense increase in the supply of the metals which are used not only as coin, but to perform the functions of money even when uncoined, and the prohibition of the coinage of silver *on private account* was much more a consequence than the cause of its depreciation.

IX.

THE DECLINE OF PRICES.

THE particular feature of existing conditions which has occasioned more uneasiness in the public mind than any other, is the decline in price of nearly all products, including labor, which must always be counted as a commodity in considering economic questions, during the last twenty-five years. This has not always been uniform during this period, nor have wages and other products always declined in the same ratio. The disturbing influence of war, a greatly depreciated currency, the drain of military service on the labor-supply, and other similar causes, naturally affected the question of prices very seriously during the entire decade 1861–71, because such great disturbance of the normal conditions of supply and demand is not immediately removed by cessation of the disturbing cause. It is unquestionable, however, that since the latter date there has been a general depreciation of nearly all values as well as of silver, which has no doubt been quite unprecedented in the history of our country. The advocates of unrestricted silver-coinage declare that this is, in the main, due to the demonetization of silver. We have shown that the depreciation of silver was due, in large part at least, to another cause—the marvellous increase in the production of coin-metal since 1849. We come now to consider the question whether the decline of prices was in any considerable degree produced by the demonetization of silver.

The first question that presents itself is, How could such demonetization affect the price of other products? To this the answer is, that it reduced the volume of the currency and thereby increased the purchasing power of gold. It is, therefore, insisted that the removal of this restriction will increase the amount of the circulating medium and thereby enhance prices.

The force of this argument depends very largely on the answers that may be given to two questions : (1) Has the restriction of silver coinage in the United States resulted in a reduction of the volume of the currency? (2) Does an increase of the volume of the currency necessarily result in an enhancement of prices? In considering the first of these questions, we are confronted at the outset with the singular, and to many no doubt startling fact, that the demonetization of silver in the United States not only has not resulted in reducing the volume of the currency, but in its actual enlargement, both in the aggregate and in its per capita ratio to the population of the country. The following table, taken from the estimates of the Secretary of the Treasury, makes this clear :

AMOUNT OF CURRENCY IN THE TREASURY AND IN CIRCU-
LATION.

IN THE TREASURY.	IN CIRCULATION.	PER CAPITA IN CIRCULATION.
1873—$ 22,563,000	$ 751,881,000	$18.04
1879— 232,889,000	818,631,000	16.75
1895— 612,932,000	1,604,131,000	22.96

All estimates in regard to the amount of currency in circulation are necessarily based on certain assumptions which can never be said to be exact. One of the chief causes of variance is as to the force to be given to the word "circulation." One class of experts make it include all money that has been put into circulation, less exports, estimated losses, and the amount in the Treasury. Another class insists on deducting from this amount the sums held by banks, insurance and loan and trust companies as reserves. There are also varying estimates of the amounts of "lost money," both coins, bank-notes, and treasury-notes. These latter are quantities which can never be determined. Senator Vest estimates that $250,000,000 of gold has been lost, by unnoted exportation and otherwise, since 1873; $20,000,000 of silver coins and $55,000,000 of United States notes and treasury-notes, and $1,400,000 treasury-notes of 1890, making $332,400,000—which he claims have been "lost," or in some manner have slipped out of the country or out

5

of existence without record, in twenty-two years ! These
are curious questions. Any man can make guesses at
them and then argue from his guesses. There has been
too much such argument upon the currency question. It
is always amusing, sometimes instructive, but at best can
only be accepted as " evidence of things hoped for."
The expert's testimony must always be estimated not
only by his intelligence, but by his opportunity and
bias.

There are certain unquestionable facts, however,
which show that there has been not a restriction but
a positive and decided increase of our currency since
1873, to wit :

1.—We have now outstanding (July 1, 1896) $98,000-
000 legal-tender treasury-notes of 1890 ; $33,400,000
currency-certificates and $336,300,000, silver-certificates
making $467,700,000, of credit-money, which was not in
existence in 1873, every dollar of which resulted from
the efforts of the government to uphold the parity of
value of silver after 1879.

2.—We have in the Treasury (July 1, 1896) $378,000-
000 silver dollars coined since 1879, which cannot be
put in circulation because no creditor of the government
wants them.

3.—We have also in the Treasury, $155,600,000 legal-
tender notes of the government and $11,400,000 silver-
certificates, or, leaving out of consideration the United
States notes, we have in the Treasury now $45,800,000,
of credit-money of the United States issued since 1879.

Now the whole amount of money, of all sorts, in the United States, in 1873, including specie and credit-money in the Treasury, according to the report of the Secretary of the Treasury was $774,445,000. To this we have added since 1879, in silver coinage, currency-certificates and silver-certificates, $778,500,000. These facts cannot be " guessed " away, and they abundantly sustain the proposition that the demonetization of silver has not reduced the currency and such reduction *cannot*, there-fore, have been the cause of the general decline in prices.

As to the second inquiry, Does an increase of the currency necessarily result in an enhancement of values?" there has long been an active controversy between two great classes of economic writers. Their disagreement is perhaps largely a matter of temperament. The great difficulty seems to be the impossibility of eliminating the effects of currency-inflation from the influence of other attending causes of appreciated values. Take the case of our own experience. It is not sufficient, in order to ar-rive at a reliable conclusion, to reduce the prices of staples to gold-equivalency during the period of inflation during and soon after the War of the Rebellion, strike an average, and say that the result is the effect of an inflated currency. Averages are delusive things at best. The average wealth of a hundred men may be $10,000 ; but one man may be worth $999,000 and the others have only $1,000 all to-gether. The average of wealth is all right, but it does not represent the average condition. So in the case in hand, the average of prices contains certain elements of inflation not resulting from an abundant currency. War created an abnormal demand for some of the staples and an abnormal scarcity of others. It took two millions of men out of the ranks of labor ; created an exceptional demand for iron, provisions, clothing, and other military supplies, all of which were subject to great waste and destruction, and greatly restricted the supply of cotton and naval stores. No skill can eliminate or define the force of these elements of our inflated prices during that time.

I am inclined to the belief that, taken by itself, a greatly increased currency of *stable* character tends to increase values by stimulating business and increasing consumption, especially of that greatest of all staples, labor. It is to be noted, however, that the only reliable instances we have of a sudden increase of a perfectly *stable* currency, which are not affected by other influences tending to modify the supply or demand for staple products, seem to have resulted in checking further depression by restoring confidence, rather than in any permanent advance of prices. These are the increased issues of legal-tender Bank of England notes, and the issue of clearing-house certificates in the cities of the United States. It is not deemed necessary to discuss this question further, however, since a way will hereafter be pointed out by which any desirable increase of the currency may, as is believed, be secured without risk of depreciation or any change in the existing stand-

ard of equivalency. To what extent even such an increase of the medium of exchange would enhance values
the writer is not prepared to say.

There is another force which has been at work in the
depression of prices to which too little weight has been
given in the consideration of this question. Just a hundred years ago, Malthus put forth, or at least developed
and expanded, a theory which has had a remarkable
effect on the economic thought of the world through
its conscious or unconscious acceptance by almost all
writers and thinkers on politico-economic subjects. It
has been especially delusive in its effects upon American
thought, since it has led us to regard our industrial and
economic conditions as too greatly affected by our own
financial conditions and legislative policy.

This theory of Malthus's was, in brief, that the sum of
human labor applied to the productive forces of nature
was, and must continue to be in an increasing ratio, insufficient to supply human needs. In other words, he
declared that population and the consequent demand,
especially for food-products, increased much more rapidly than the capacity of the world to supply them.
Since that time, science and invention have been applied
to production, transportation, the preservation of products, and the restriction of consumption, to such an
extent that it is probable that the general productive
capacity of the laborer has been increased tenfold—it
may be even more—in its relation to consumption. In
the first place, the capacity of the soil itself has been

astonishingly increased by the adoption of scientific methods and the use of scientific fertilizers. The application of machinery to agricultural processes, plowing, sowing, reaping, threshing, has many times increased the individual capacity to produce and reduced in an almost corresponding ratio, the consumption on which demand depends. Improvements in methods of preservation, such as canning and cold storage, have amazingly restricted waste. The substitution of non-consuming motors, steam and electricity, for the horse, have in a still greater degree increased the ability to market the world's products without waste, and, at the same time, restricted consumption by reducing the number of laborers required to move a specified tonnage, while almost wholly eliminating the consumption of food-products by animate motors—in other words, the consumption of agricultural products by draft animals once employed in transporting the world's production.

In the field of manufacturing production the operation of these forces has been even more marked and wonderful. One man's labor in the production of steel and the grosser steel fabrics, is to-day easily equivalent to that of a hundred men a hundred years ago. Possibly it may be even in excess of that ratio. So, also, in the manufacture of textile fabrics, of clothing, shoes, and other necessary articles ; one man's labor supplemented by machinery, improved processes, and the economics of aggregated production, results in an output at least a score of times as great as was possible before their introduction. The

result of these conditions is that we have at length
reached the point where Malthus's theory becomes evidently false, not in degree only but in its essential, fundamental idea. The world's labor applied to the production
of the necessaries of life for any specific period is now
much more than sufficient to meet the world's demand for
such necessaries during a like period. The necessary
result is to increase the force of competition, restrict
the demand for labor, and reduce the margin of profit.

These influences happen to have culminated during
the last quarter of a century, following hard upon the
war-epoch of inflated prices, being coincident with the
amazing increase in the supply of coin-metal, the depreciation of silver, the experiment of legal-tender credit-
money in the United States, and the attempt to uphold
the parity of silver by enforced coinage and use as a
basis of currency at a ratio far above its commercial
value. For a time, their effect was modified or delayed
by an immense demand for railway construction and
other kinds of development which were peculiarly active
during the period immediately succeeding the close of
the war. This was followed, first by apprehension of
tariff changes which might affect the profits of production already greatly reduced by this condition, and
afterwards by the adoption of such changes which
exposed our productive industry to competition with the
surplus labor of the rest of the world on terms peculiarly
unfavorable to American producers and in the same
ratio more favorable to foreign competitors. The result

has been a great improvement in the conditions of foreign production and a more than corresponding depression of American industry, because of the culminating
effects of actual over-production, of restricted demand,
and of the doubt resulting from monetary experiments
of unprecedented extent and inherently dubious character.

X.

" VALUE," " EQUIVALENCY," " MONEY," " CREDIT."

MUCH of the confusion which exists upon this subject is believed to arise from inadequate or inexact definitions, especially of the term "value," and neglect of the distinction between it and "equivalency." "Money" and "credit" and the kinds of each also require brief consideration.

Value is the quality of *desirability*, or the degree of desirability, which an object possesses for any individual. It is not an attribute of matter like weight or dimension, but an expression of the relation that subsists between an individual consciousness and any material object or immaterial concept. It is of two kinds, appreciable and inappreciable.

Appreciable value is that desirability which may be expressed by comparison, on which a price may be set.

Inappreciable value is that which can be expressed only by contrast, which is above price or beyond measure.

Equivalency is the expression of price, or the correlative term by which *appreciable* value is expressed.

As illustrating these definitions, I may say that a bushel of apples is worth fifty cents ; that the pen with which I

write is worth a dollar ; that the sword which hangs
above my desk is *invaluable ;* that life is *beyond all price ;*
that a patriot values his country *above his life ;* or that
the Christian values the hope of immortality *above all
earthly things.*

No one would ever mistake any of these expressions
of value ; but when one comes to attempt to explain
the cause, origin, or source of such concept, that is,
on what common quality of " apples," " pen," " sword,"
" life," " country," and " hope of immortality," the
" value " attributed to each depends, he simply under-
takes to define the indefinable. Value is merely an
expression of *desirability,* and the *causes* of desirability
are infinite and constantly varying with time, location,
distance, or other conditions.

In the above instances, I say the bushel of apples is
worth fifty cents because that is the price at which they
can be bought or sold ; the pen is worth a dollar because
I would have to pay that sum to get another of like
quality, or think I would.   But the sword—why should
that be " invaluable," that is, *beyond* price ?   It is only
a bit of steel with a battered scabbard and a brass hilt
engraved with a few battle-names.   It never was of any
use, except once, and then only for a fraction of a
minute.   To another it would be "worth" nothing
now.   Threaten me or my loved ones with want and I
would sell it for a loaf.   That is, what is an inappreciable value to-day, without any change in its character
may become an appreciable value to-morrow.   So, too,

"value" may depend altogether on location. A fur coat may be worthless in the tropics and worth a fortune in the arctic regions. In Samaria, when the city was besieged, a pint of dove's dung was worth five pieces of silver. A bow-shot away, outside the walls, it not only was worth nothing, but its possession meant defilement. Value, whether appreciable or inappreciable, depends wholly upon the relation of the individual to the thing to which value is attributed.

The trouble with many of the definitions of value which are used by economic writers is that they are attempts to define or limit the origin or source of values, rather than to make clear the real nature of the concept. Thus, some have endeavored to maintain that all appreciable values are the result of labor or depend upon the utility of the objects to which value is attributed. Such definitions, coming afterwards to be used as premises, have led not only to confusion but to infinite mischief in economic speculation.

Appreciable values are expressed either by comparison of one specific value with another or in terms of some fixed and generally accepted system of equivalency. The former is called barter; the latter trade or exchange.

Money is any graduated system of equivalency established by law and represented in whole or in part by visible symbols provided by law, which are used in ordinary exchange at their prescribed equivalency and receivable at that rate in payment of debts.

A monetary system, is composed of two elements : (1) A legally established denominational scale of abstract equivalencies ; (2) legally prescribed material symbols representing some or all the denominations of such graduated scale.

Money is of two kinds : Coin and credit-money.

Coins are portions of precious metal, of prescribed weight, form, and fineness, the *values* of which are legally declared to be *equivalent* to specific denominations of any particular monetary system, the weight of the various coins being determined by a *unit of equivalency* and all other coins of the same material being multiples or fractions of its weight and of the same fineness or an equivalent alloy. The unit of equivalency is sometimes termed the " standard of value "; it is really the standard of equivalency only. Money does not fix or determine values, but expresses them when fixed in the mind of buyer or seller.

The value of all money is regulated by the general desirability of the metal of which the symbol representing the unit of equivalency is composed, and this value varies with the relation which the demand for this metal bears to the supply of coin-metal, as we have already seen.

What is termed a *double-standard* or a *bimetallic*-standard is a monetary system in which *specific* amounts of two metals are legally declared to be equal to each other in value and of like equivalency. The difference in the weight of the two symbols representing the unit of equivalency in such a system is said to be the *ratio of equivalency* of the two metals. If the one symbol is sixteen times heavier than the other having the same equivalency, the ratio is 16 to 1. When the value, that is, the general desirability of the metal composing one of the units of equivalency in such a monetary system, comes to exceed that of the other, the most valuable coinage ceases to be regarded as money, and becomes a commodity. Its *equivalency* remains the same, being determined by law, so that it will only pay the same amount of debt, if used as money ; but its *value* or general desirability being greater than that of its co-ordinate symbol, it will buy more if used in exchange. So the man who has it will sell it as he would any other commodity, and pay his debts with the less valuable symbol. This is what is meant by " Gresham's Law," as it is termed, that " poor money drives out good money." A difference in the *value* of coins of the same equivalency reduces the unit of equivalency to the value of the least desirable, and by making the more desirable symbol a commodity drives it out of circulation as money.

Credit-money is any system of denominational promises to pay coin, regulated by law, which are legal-tenders for any debt not specifically stated to be payable in some other form of currency. It is of two kinds—(1) that issued by a government itself ; (2) that issued by a bank to which the authority to emit notes having the legal-tender quality has been granted by a government as a profitable concession. The United States notes (green-backs) and the treasury-notes of 1890 are examples of the former class ; the notes of the Bank of England, the Bank of France, the Imperial Bank of Germany, and the national banks of Sweden, Norway, and some other countries, are examples of the second.

Substitute-money is any system of legally regulated promises to pay coin, or some legal equivalent, which circulates by common consent but is *not* a legal-tender for debts. This is the ordinary status of what is called " bank-currency." The great trouble with it is that it fails to serve the purposes of money when most needed ; it is accepted in payment of debts when times are good and refused as soon as they become bad. The notes of our National banks belong, technically, in this class,—but, as they are payable in coin or legal-tender promises of the United States, and these *legal-tenders* are redeemable in gold, they are really equivalent to legal-tender of the government.

Token-money is an apparent exception to the definitions above given. It consists of coins having little or no intrinsic value, which are used to represent fractions of the unit of equivalency too small to be represented by coins made of precious metals. They are kept in circulation by the necessity that exists for small change, by limitation of amount, by restriction of use or limited legal-tender quality, and by the fact that each person's interest in their purchasing power, whether it be more or less, is so small as to be of little consequence.

Currency is a term used to include all forms of money and all denominational promises to pay money. Its use as a synonym of money alone, has led to some confusion in popular thought. The use of the terms "paper-money" and "paper-currency" have tended to increase this confusion of thought by diverting attention from the real element of value, which is, in all cases, *the value of the promise to pay*. The *equivalency* of coin and credit-money is the same, but the *value* of the former depends on the desirability of the material of which it is composed, while the value of the latter depends on the reliability of the promise of which it consists : the value of the material on which it may be impressed has nothing to do with it.

Credit-*currency* has been an important instrument of exchange ever since the establishment of banks of issue ; credit-*money* has become an important element of currency only since the grant of legal-tender quality to Bank of England notes sixty years ago, to the notes of the Bank of France a few years later, to the demand-notes of the United States in 1862, and to the issues of several of the banks of other European nations since that time.

Thus far, our credit-money has consisted of the promise of the government to pay coin *on demand*. This the government has properly and wisely construed to be a promise to pay gold when the holder preferred it to silver. The abandonment of the policy of requiring customs duties to be paid in gold, left the Treasury without means to secure gold coin to meet this demand, except by issuing bonds and selling them for gold. By this means the bonded debt has been already increased $262,000,000, with an existing deficiency approximating $40,000,000 more. This amount at four per cent. interest, the bonds having thirty years to run, represents an increase of the annual interest-charge of the government of $12,000,000, amounting in thirty years to $360,000,000 in gold in addition to the principal of the bond.

This process seems likely to continue until the entire credit-currency of the United States is retired from circulation and the bonded debt proportionately increased. The amount of demand-currency outstanding July 1, 1896, amounted to $352,508,000, the interest on which would be in four per cent. bonds, $14,000,000 a year, which in thirty years would amount to $420,000,000. To this should properly be added the outstanding silver-certificates, amounting to $331,259,000 more, making the whole principal $584,000,000.

Two methods have been proposed for obviating the evils of our present monetary system :

(1) The unrestricted coinage of silver on private account, which would at once place the whole demand-currency of the United States on a silver basis, and reduce the purchasing power of the same 47 per cent. As this constitutes more than one half of the money actually in use in business at this time, this would mean a loss in purchasing power of nearly one half in more than half the money the people hold. The

loss would fall, of course, most heavily on the poorer classes, to whom their little store on hand is like the widow's mite—all that they have. It is a proposition hardly paralleled for cold-blooded injustice in all the world's history.

(2) The alternative proposition, in the several forms in which it has been stated, is to extend or modify our present system of National Banks, giving them a monopoly, actual or resultant, of the issue of credit-currency, to be based on bonds of the United States, and their ultimate redemption to be guaranteed by the United States.

This is infinitely preferable to the other, but is open to the objection of cost, already pointed out, and certain other objections which imperatively suggest the inquiry whether a better and cheaper method is not possible, and whether, under existing conditions at least, it is not preferable. This consideration has induced the formulation of the plan set forth in the next chapter.

6

XI

NATIONAL CURRENCY AND NATIONAL CREDIT.

IN all civilized countries the relation between national credit and national currency is one of constantly increasing intimacy and importance. Indeed, it may be truthfully said that the financial and monetary progress of the last fifty years, which has been much greater than was made in centuries before, has been mainly along the line of increased use and greater certainty of private credit and the perfection of public credit, especially by the reduction of the rate of interest on national indebtedness and its employment to supplement coinage as an essential element of national currency. No one influence has tended so steadily and strongly to appreciate the public credit of the leading nations of the world and to promote the stability of their respective currencies as the intimate and vital relations that have been established between the two, and in nothing else is the financial and monetary progress of the age so clearly apparent as in the development and extension of these relations.

The chief element in this remarkable improvement in monetary methods has been the substitution of actual credit-money having full legal-tender quality, for *substi*-

tute-money or a banking-currency having no adequate basis of stability, but dependent on accident for its hold on public confidence, subject to frequently recurring waves of public distrust, and always proving weakest and most variable when there was most need of strength, uniformity, and stability. This movement has manifested itself in three forms : (1) In the grant of the legal-tender quality to the notes of great banking institutions which are so intimately connected with their various governments as really to constitute an integral part of their financial policies and administrative machinery. One hundred and twenty years ago this very year, Adam Smith called attention to the fact that the Bank of England was something more than a great banking corporation, being, in fact, a most essential part of the government itself. How close and indissoluble this relation was even then, is apparent from the wonder and perplexity which shows in his attempt to analyze and define the same. But the directors of that most famous of all financial institutions would have been stricken dumb with amazement if they could have foreseen the strengthening of the bond that now unites the " Old Lady of Threadneedle Street " with the destinies of the British Empire, to the evident and inestimable advantage of both. This closer union resulted chiefly from the act of 1832, by which her control of the fiscal resources of the realm was greatly extended and her issues were made a legal-tender for all debts public and private. By the act of 1844 this fiscal union was made more complete by absolute control of receipts and expenditures of the government and the entire administration of the public debt. The revenues and the credit of the Empire are practically in her control, and $80,000,000 of her issues are based solely on the public credit. She has also control of the sinking-fund of the government. Because of this, she is the Gibraltar of the nation's credit and is in turn sustained by it.

In France the same course has been pursued. The issues of the Bank of France were made legal-tender in 1838, and her fiscal relations with the government are even more vital, especially since 1874, no other banking institution being allowed to issue denominational notes. Germany and Austria, Norway and Sweden have adopted substantially the same policy. The result is an unexampled stability of credit-currency. In the United States the experiment was first made of a banking-system based on the credit of the government but not legal-tender, though the redemption of the issues is guaranteed by the government.

(2) Here too has been tried for the first time on any great scale, the experiment of a legal-tender currency issued directly by the government and redeemable at all times on demand in gold coin; or, to state it more accurately, in any coin of the realm the holder chooses to designate. This currency has been subject to much criticism. For seventeen years it was objected that it was not redeemed according to its terms. During the past three years it has been made evident that its con-

stant redeemability can only be maintained by a constant increase of the bonded debt in order to secure gold to meet such demand. The result has been vexatious, unsatisfactory, and costly, as we have already shown. This experience inclines one, naturally, to inquire why the issue of a legal-tender credit-currency under authority of government and based largely on its credit, which has proved the sheet-anchor of stability in other countries when made indirectly by a fiscal agent of the government, should have failed here when made directly by the government itself.

In considering the reasons for this difference, we are confronted at the outset with the astonishing fact that through all the unprecedented monetary conditions of the last quarter of a century the terminal-credit of the country—that is, its interest-bearing obligations having a specific term and payable in gold—have been worth more than gold from the day of issue to the day of payment. Considered by itself this result is not remarkable. In the first place, they are payable in that money which thus far in the world's history has shown the least depreciation, to wit : gold. In the next place, the resources of the United States exceed those of any other government, and have not been depleted by long-continued exhausting demands. And in the third place, the United States has established a reputation as a debt-paying nation unparalleled by any other country. Others have refunded greater sums and braced their credit with those visible appeals to public confidence known as sinking-funds of one sort and another, to a greater degree, but none has such a magnificent record of debt actually paid off and discharged within a like period by the actual application of surplus revenues, alone. At the risk of wearying the reader, there is appended here what it was the author's fixed purpose to avoid in this work—a table. He believes that, as a rule, statistical tables lead to confusion and weariness of the ordinary reader. They are the armories from which the student of social and economic problems draws his facts, but the duty of the economic writer who addresses himself to a popular audience is usually to use these facts rather than invite his readers to inspect the magazines from which they are drawn. This record is such an incredible one, so well deserving universal consideration as a sound basis of patriotic pride, that an exception is gladly made in its favor. It ought to be made an object-lesson in every school-house in the land, to impress on the minds of coming generations the essential honesty of the American people and their manly restiveness under the burden of obligation to those who lent a helping hand in the hour of the country's sorest need.

A QUARTER CENTURY OF DEBT-PAYING.

	TOTAL INTEREST-BEARING DEBT.	٭ ANNUAL INTEREST-CHARGE
1869......	$2,162,060,522 39	$125,523,998 34
1870......	2,046,455,722 39	118,784,960 34
1871......	1,934,696,750 00	11ſ,949,330 50
1872......	1,814,794,100 00	103,988,463 00
1873......	1,710,483,950 00	98,049,804 00
1874......	1,738,930,750 00	98,796,004 50
1875......	1,722,676,300 00	96,855,690 50
1876......	1,710,685,450 00	95,104,269 00
1877......	1,711,888,500 00	93,160,643 50
1878......	1,794,735,650 00	94,654,472 50
1879......	1,797,643,700 00	83,773,778 50
1880......	1,723,993,100 00	79,633,981 00
1881......	1,639,567,750 00	٭ 75,018,695 50
1882......	1,463,810,400 00	57,300,110 75
1883......	1,338,229,150 00	51,436,709 50
1884......	1,226,563,850 00	47,926,432 50
1885......	1,196,150,950 00	47,014,133 00
1886......	1,146,014,100 00	45,510,098 00
1887......	1,021,692,350 00	41,780,529 00
1888......	950,522,500 00	38,991,935 25
1889......	829,853,990 00	33,752,354 60
1890......	725,313,110 00	29,417,603 15
1891......	610,529,120 00	23,615,735 80
1892......	585,029,330 00	22,893,883 20

What are the central facts of this record? $1,577,
031,192.39 of public debt paid off, cancelled, and wiped
out in twenty-four consecutive years! An average of
more than $65,000,000 each year! Also a reduction of
the yearly interest-charge in that time of $102,630,115.14,
or an average of $4,276,254 a year. No wonder the

world wants our bonds and is willing to pay a premium for them !

But in the face of this, why is it that our demand-notes have given us so much trouble? In what respect do they differ from our bonds? In just three things :

1.—They are constantly demandable, instead of being payable at a particular time.

2.—They do not bear interest.

3.—They are a legal-tender for debts, while the bonds are not.

It is evident that the last-named element of difference cannot exert any depreciating influence, but rather the reverse ; an interest-bearing-bond having a specific time to run or payable at a fixed date, would be enhanced rather than deteriorated by having the legal-tender quality attached to it. The second, the fact that they are not interest-bearing obligations, is an evident reason why they should rank in desirability below those that are ; but it is not a sufficient reason why the promise of so abundantly solvent a debtor should be so eagerly exchanged for gold which is also non-interest-bearing. Is there anything in the nature of the demand-notes or the conditions of the times that will explain this fact?

There are certain facts which not only fully explain this variance, but the mere statement of which itself makes evident that it should exist : (1) The fact of constant redeemability. The whole world has an instinctive perception of the falsity of this theory. (2) The fact that since the abandonment of the policy of having import duties paid in gold, it has been evident that there is no legal provision for maintaining the gold reserve to meet even an ordinary demand except by borrowing or rather buying gold. (3) The world has taken note of our prolonged and remarkably variegated struggle to preserve the parity of silver coin with gold at the ratio of sixteen to one and compel the use of a large silver-coinage as currency under those conditions. (4) The world knows that while a nation with such a record for debt-paying as ours would never default in the interest, or fail to provide for paying the principal of its bonds, the infatuation for a particular monetary theory might possibly lead it to attempt the dangerous and absurd experiment of paying in a depreciated coinage a demand-obligation in which the form of the currency to be used in its redemption was not specifically stated.

Because of these things, the demand-obligations of the government have been well designated "an endless chain," the constant use of which is to draw gold from the Treasury which can only be replenished by new loans.

This tendency to exchange our legal-tender notes for gold has been greatly strengthened by a just apprehension on the part of the obligors in maturing gold-contracts that complications are likely to arise which might render it difficult to obtain gold to meet such obligations, and, also, by the just and proper caution on the part of managers of institutions which are required to keep an available reserve fund—such as banks, insurance and trust companies—who, while entertaining perhaps no serious doubt of the ultimate redemption of the government's promises to pay, clearly perceive the difficulty of maintaining the continuous redeemability of our demand-notes, and deem it the part of wisdom as trustees of great interests to reduce their holdings of legal-tender credit-money and increase their reserve of gold. Under the circumstances, this was an act of common prudence and discretion on the part of both these classes. The result has been, while greatly stimulating the demand for gold, to wholly withdraw the same from circulation, so that the entire stock of gold in the country at this time is held either as reserves of this sort, to meet possible contingencies of gold-debtors, or in anticipation of speculative opportunity to arise from possible further impairment of our currency by free-silver agitation. This situation has been very properly pronounced unbearable. No honest man of sincere patriotism desires it to continue. The result of all these conditions has been to create three distinct phases of public sentiment in regard to our future monetary policy.

The restriction of the circulation by the retirement of gold and the depression caused by the attempt to sustain the parity of silver by putting the government's credit behind our silver-coinage through an immense certification of it, intensified by the restriction of production by apprehended and actual tariff modifications, has created a widespread conviction that the great need of the present time is more money—and immediate and decided increase of the currency—which it is hoped would result in stimulating enterprise and enlarging the field of profitable production, increase the demand for labor, raise the rate of wages, and, by these means if not otherwise, enable the debtor more easily to discharge his obligations. To this element of our people a lack of sufficient currency seems the chief evil of our present monetary conditions, and they are willing to run the risk of a depreciated currency to remedy it. This is the position, fairly stated, of the great majority of those who propose as a remedy the unrestricted coinage of silver. More money and cheaper money, even at the risk of deterioration in its quality, is the position they occupy in regard to our currency.

Another class, more conservative and cautious, but not less sincere and patriotic, believing that stability and uniformity of value and equivalency between all parts of our currency is the matter of prime importance, demand as a first step the retirement of our entire credit-currency by the immediate issue of bonds, leaving the future situation to take care of itself.

Another class, recognizing the inconsistency of demanding the retirement of $600,000,000 of credit-currency, which constitutes more than half—probably two-thirds—of the actual circulation since the withdrawal or occlusion of gold, without proposing some feasible method for readily supplying the place of the same, while joining in the demand for the retirement of our credit-currency, propose the establishment of some system of banks of issue, the notes of which shall be based wholly or in part upon the credit of the government and their redemption guaranteed by it, but without legal-tender quality.

This latter proposition is sure to encounter serious opposition. The temper of the popular mind in regard to the predominant power of corporations, trusts, and similar aggregations of capital in shaping our political, financial, and industrial conditions, would inevitably take alarm at the prospect of putting the entire credit-currency of the country in the control of a system of banking institutions which, by concerted action, would have the power to increase or diminish the supply, to raise the rate of interest, and, in short, as was charged against the old United States Bank, "to kill and make alive, to destroy whom they wished to render powerless, and to uphold whom they desired to see prosper." It is a matter for serious consideration whether such a course, imposing as it inevitably would a great increase of taxation, would not greatly inflame the already dangerously popular sentiment that there is an "irrepressible conflict" between the rich and poor in this country. There is no doubt that the "greenback," in its thirty-four years of existence as an important part of our currency, has made a very deep and favorable impression on the public mind, and the demand that the government shall supply a sufficient currency without the intervention of any system of banks of issue is by no means restricted within party lines. The only question to be decided is whether such a currency is compatible with stability and uniformity of value, and can be made secure from dangerous fluctuations. These facts are confidently relied upon as excuse for the suggestion offered in the next chapter.

Credit is a not less important instrument of exchange than money. It is said that more than nine-tenths, perhaps ninety-nine hundredths, of the monetary transactions of the country are effected, somewhere in the course of their development, with this element. Its actual extent can never be determined. It is the product of confidence; expands with prosperity and shrinks with depression. The contraction of credit produces the impression of a scarcity of money, even when there has been no change whatever in the volume of currency. Credit is of two kinds, terminal and demandable. Terminal credit is any form of obligation that is payable at a certain time; demandable credit is that which is payable at the call of the creditor. Credit is also, as to its character, interest-bearing and non-interest-bearing. As an element of the currency, credit has been used chiefly in the form of non-interest-bearing denominational demand-notes. These may be either legal-tender or not. The United States notes and treasury-notes of 1890 are legal-tenders, the currency and silver-certificates are not. All are demand-obligations, however, and are therefore subject to the distrust which naturally attaches to a pledge of "constant redeemability" in any specific medium, when the amount of the medium of redemption evidently falls greatly below the amount of circulation to be redeemed.

"*Constant redeemability*" is a device originally intended, and still chiefly used, to enhance the profits of banks of issue. It consists of an attempt to make a part continuously equal to the whole. It depends upon the theory that bank-notes, or credit-currency of any sort, to a specific amount, having once been put in circulation, can be kept redeemable on presentation by holding in reserve a much smaller sum, say one-third the amount of the issue, in coin, relying on the skill of the banker, the accident of wide dispersion of the bills, and the use of deposits to make good whatever demand there may be at any particular time above the amount of this reserve.

The principle of "constant redeemability" is of course fallacious, as even a child may see at a glance. In sporting parlance it would properly be termed a "bluff."

It depends for its success wholly on the impression made on the popular mind by an *apparent* ability to comply with the terms of the vaunt. If the power to redeem happens to outlast a particular attack of public distrust, well and good ; if it does not, the crash comes, the public loses, and the old see-saw game of confidence and panic goes on again, perhaps with new players, but in the same way and always with the same ultimate result, because its essential element, "constant redeemability" is a constant lie.

The danger of such revulsions has been greatly

mitigated by the grant of legal-tender quality to the issues of those great banking institutions which are really a part of the governments under whose authority they act.

When a *government* promises to redeem in gold an amount of credit-money which every one knows it has not gold enough to redeem if it should be demanded, it has none of the gambler's advantage which enables a bank to stand up to its "bluff." The public does not know the actual resources of a bank—how much gold it really has or how much it may be able to secure while it delays the demand by paying, as the Bank of England sometimes has been compelled to do, forty shillings in silver to each demandant; that being the limit within which silver is a legal tender in Great Britain. Even with that advantage and the support of the powerful government of which it is really a part, and on whose securities it issues legal-tender notes to the value of about $100,000,000, its bullion has sometimes been drawn upon almost to exhaustion, and but for the aid of the Bank of France it must have closed its doors. "Constant redeemability" is a confidence-game in which ignorance of a bank's actual condition, resources, and means of obtaining temporary assistance, are most important elements.

When a government, especially one of restricted powers and represented by officials whose powers are not only strictly defined but must be exercised in the glare of publicity, attempts to play this game, it does so at an evident disadvantage. It is like playing with an antagonist who knows one's hand. Everybody is aware just how much gold the Treasury holds and what chance there is to replenish it. So the pretence of "constant-redeemability" is an apparent farce. A reserve of $100,000,000 has proved insufficient to keep $340,000,000 of greenbacks in circulation. Again and again, the holders of them have come and asked for gold. Why? Not because the credit of the government is not the best in the world, but because the demand for gold everywhere—to meet gold-contracts in this country and to serve as redemption-money for credit-currency abroad —has increased its *desirability* beyond that represented by the treasury-notes or the silver-certificates for which it is exchangeable.

As the result of our experiment in trying to keep the desirability of 412½ grains of standard silver equal to 25⅘ grains of standard gold, by making credit-currency " constantly redeemable " in either gold or silver coin at the creditor's option, we have kept an average of about $130,000,000 of gold lying idle in the treasury for twenty years, have had to borrow over $260,000,000 more at 4 per cent. interest, the bonds running thirty years, and are at this date (August 1, 1896) only saved from entire depletion of the Treasury by the grace of a syndicate of foreign bankers and domestic capitalists who have *" agreed to protect the gold-reserve in the Treasury until after the election !"*

Truly, the situation is most humiliating and shameful ! A combination of capitalists volunteering to hold up our national credit and save the United States from bankruptcy !

But how can such a situation be remedied ? Not by trying to increase the value—that is, let it be remembered always, the *desirability* of our silver coins by increasing the number of them a hundred fold—but by applying to our credit-money the same principle which makes our bonds at this very moment worth fifteen or twenty per cent. more than gold. It is enough to make any one laugh who can refrain from tears, to see a great nation, whose promise to pay gold thirty years hence is *worth one-fifth more than its face in gold coin*, forced to solicit individuals to help us make good our boasts of "constant *redeemability*" and "*parity of value*" between our gold and silver coinage ! It is the self-evident absurdity of such claims which inclines men to accept almost any proposal, no matter how ridiculous it may be, that shall promise a remedy. One does not need to be a financier, nor even to have studied the currency question very profoundly, to understand that a man, a corporation, or a country, whose *terminal-credit* sells in the world's market at from twelve to twenty per cent. above par, can only be in such straits as the Treasury now is with regard to its *demand-promises*, from two causes :

1. Failure to provide means by which to obtain gold to meet them without borrowing ; or,

2. Failure to employ the same or similar means to enhance their desirability as have been used to maintain its *terminal*-credit.

7

XII.

TERMINAL LEGAL-TENDER CREDIT-MONEY.

Is it possible to give to our credit-currency the same desirability, in character if not in degree, that now attaches to our bonds? If it is, the problems of our present monetary situation are readily solved, the demand for an increase of the currency may then be safely and easily met, and the counter-demand for stability, elasticity, and uniformity of value between all its elements abundantly satisfied.

In considering this question, it is necessary to keep in mind these facts : (1) That a credit-currency *always* maintains an exact equivalency with the coin in which it is payable, so long as the credit of the promisor is good. (2) That the entire debt of the United States— that is, the sum of all its promises to pay—amounts at this time to about $1,900,000,000. Of this debt about $900,000,000 bears no interest and consists, in the main, of demand-obligations of one sort and another. (3) That the retirement of the demand-obligations by the issue of an equivalent amount of bonds at present rates would immensely increase the interest-charge of the country. (4) That if the same can be safely transmuted into credit-currency, it will at once relieve the gold-reserve and save the interest upon at least $100,000,000 idle funds which we have had to pay for twenty years in and to maintain our pledge to perform two impossible things—viz., make our demand-notes always redeemable and preserve parity of value between our coins. (5) That the demand-obligations constitute a debt which must be paid at some time and in some manner.

If it is possible to fund our demand-obligations at one per cent. and at the same time transform them into a stable currency always equal in value with gold, without any modification of the present standard, without risk of panic or depreciation of values, but on the contrary with an assured increase of confidence and resulting stimulation of business, it is surely a consummation devoutly to be wished. The belief that all this is not only possible but very easy of attainment alone induces the author to submit the following considerations to all who are not so blinded by the conflict between two ideas as to forget that the ultimate end to be attained is not the predominance of any particular theory, but the fulfilment of the sentiment recently expressed by Mr. Chauncey Depew that "this country ought to have the best currency in the world."

If the free-coinage of silver should prevail, our currency will at once fall to the level of the *worst* in the world. If we retire the demand-notes and supply their place with a bank-currency, it will be at least *no better* than other nations have. Let us see if an actually *better* currency is not attainable.

We have already seen that the disparity between our *demand*-obligations and our *terminal*-credit is due to two things : (1) the fact that the bonds bear interest and (2) that one has greater confidence in an obligation payable at a fixed time than he can have in any pledge of "constant-redeemability." Suppose now, we should remove this disparity by changing our demand-obligations into terminal, interest-bearing, denominational issues of a like amount and having in addition thereto the legal-tender quality.

Or, to be more specific, suppose we issue denominational legal-tender currency to the amount of our present demand-obligations, bearing one per cent. interest, renewable with payment of accrued interest in gold coin after five years, dividing the same into five classes, so as to make one-fifth of the whole renewable each year, and making a certain portion of the whole, say *one-fiftieth*, redeemable in gold each year. What would be the result?

The legal-tender quality would certainly not detract from the value of such issues regarded as terminal-credit obligations.

The rate of interest is not high enough in connection with the short-term limit, five years, to lead them to be sought as speculative investments except during the fifth year.

They would become especially desirable as reserves for insurance companies, trust-companies, and similar institutions, instead of gold, because of their interest-bearing quality, and their substitution for gold would release this to meet existing gold contracts.

The holders of non-legal-tender obligations of the government would prefer them because of their legal-tender quality.

The holders of all our non-interest-bearing obligations would prefer them because they would bear interest.

It would at once eliminate all questions concerning "parity of value," except as regards the small amount of silver coin now actually in circulation and the coin now in the Treasury. This could very safely be left to settle itself, as the substitution of this currency would call in all the small denominations of our credit-money and leave the field of small change to be filled exclusively by silver according to the intent of existing laws.

From these considerations it will be seen that the change can be made at once, without compulsion but by direct appeal to the self-interest of holders of our demand-obligations, without any restriction of the currency, without any possible panic or stringency, and with the consequences of making our whole currency immediately and unquestionably equal with gold.

But let us go a little further. All this constitutes a debt to be paid, unless after a time it should be decided to continue some portion of it as a permanent loan such as other nations' debts mostly are. Leaving this out of consideration for the present, let us consider how the gradual payment of the debt might be effected. Suppose we say that *one-fiftieth* of the whole amount shall be paid each year. This will make the sum that may be demanded at the Treasury each year consist of two elements : (1) Interest on one-fifth of the whole amount payable in gold coin. (2) One-fiftieth of the whole amount of principal payable in gold coin.

Suppose, for convenience of estimate merely, that the whole amount was one billion dollars. One-fifth of this would be $200,000,000, one per cent. interest on which would be $2,000,000. The whole amount of gold which could be demanded of the Treasury in any year, under this system then, would be one-fiftieth of the principal, $20,000,000, and interest on one-fifth of it, $2,000,000, or $22,000,000, in all. The "endless chain" would be at once and forever broken.

We come now to consider the question of cost. The entire cost of $1,000,000,000 of such currency would amount to one per cent. interest, or $10,000,000 a year. This is the exact sum the government has to pay for $250,-000,000 of our present banking currency based on bonds at four per cent., leaving out of the estimate the exemption from state and municipal prevailing taxation under that system. In other words, *it would cost considerably less than one-fourth as much as an equivalent amount of banking currency based on bonds like our national bank-notes.*

It would seem to be unnecessary to go into further detail. Every reader can make his own estimates as to partial or continuing operation of this system. The arrangement of the classes is a mere matter of arithmetic. There would have to be four classes of one, two, three,

and four years' term, respectively, at first. Afterwards
they would be regularly one-fifth's, renewable each year.
To transform it into a permanent loan it would only be
necessary to offer the holder a chance to renew instead
of taking payment in gold for one-fiftieth each year.

Each class of these terminal legal-tender obligations
would have to bear the legend " Renewable with five per
cent. accrued interest payable in gold on presentation
after January 1st " of a specified year. Those of each
class made payable at the same time, which on the sched-
ule proposed would be one-tenth of each class, or one
fifthieth of the whole, would have the legend " Payable
in gold coin with five per cent. accrued interest on presentation after January 1st " of a specified year.

The only objections thus far urged to such a plan are,
(1) That it makes no provision for using our silver product as coinage. The same objection applies to all our
other products with equal force. No government can be
required to purchase any class of products because there
is not a profitable market for them otherwise. (2) That
a credit-currency can only be kept at par with gold by
the promise of " constant redeemability." This objection should need no answer to the mind of every candid
and intelligent man.

To keep our demand-issues on a par with gold on the
theory of "constant redeemability," we have been compelled to keep a gold reserve of $100,000,000 to $197,000,-
000 lying idle for twenty years. Even then we have
failed to accomplish that result and been obliged to

borrow nearly $300,000,000 more in the attempt. This
$100,000,000 gold reserve has cost, of course, the interest
on that sum, and the amount borrowed shows this sum
was insufficient. Suppose we assume that $150,000,000
would be enough. The interest on this at four per cent.
would be $6,000,000 a year. No one will claim that
this estimate is extravagant. This is the sum that must
be paid on the theory of "constant-demandability," to
keep our credit-money equal in desirability with gold.
This sum alone is equal to the cost of $600,000,000, ter-
minal-legal-tenders under the plan proposed—a greater
amount of legal-tender than we have ever had in circulation.

The ease with which this system of terminal legal-
tenders may be substituted for the bonded debt at ma-
turity is another feature which should not be left uncon-
sidered. By giving the holders of maturing bonds the
option of gold or this terminal legal-tender credit-money
it would be easy to expand the currency to any desirable
limit of need.

So far as the writer is able to perceive, this simple
and easily made change in our currency would meet
any reasonable demand for increase of volume ; would
give an assurance of stability that would at once restore
confidence ; offers the easiest possible method for re-
funding the public debt ; secures uniformity of value in
all parts of our currency ; would be the cheapest form of
credit-currency ever proposed, and would secure for
the country what Mr. Depew declared that every patriot
ought to desire, "the best currency in the world."

XIII.

THE RESULTS OF FREE-COINAGE OF SILVER.

THERE seems to be in most of the works on this subject a curious lack of systematized statement of the immediate and indubitable results of the free-coinage of silver upon existing conditions, some of which seem to have been almost wholly overlooked. The most important of these are as follows :

1. It is not to be denied that the immediate result would be to depreciate all the money now in circulation, except gold coin and gold-certificates, nearly fifty per cent. It matters not how abundant money may become or how easily it may be obtainable hereafter, one thing is beyond all question : the very day that the free-coinage of silver becomes a national policy, should such a day ever dawn, the man who goes to market with silver coin, silver-certificates, currency-certificates, treasury-notes, or national bank currency in his pocket, will find prices doubled and the purchasing power of his money only half what it now is. This is tantamount to depriving the present holders of our currency of one-half its value. As all these forms of currency amount to about *one billion dollars*, one sees that the first effect of such a

policy would be to take out of the pockets of the American people some *$500,000,000 before a single silver dollar could be coined.*

This loss would fall almost entirely upon people of small means to whom the day's or week's supply of money is of supreme importance. Between the day of the election and the inauguration of a " silver " administration, credit would have been withdrawn, and all people of large means would have prepared for the shock, and be found with little money save gold in their possession. The poor and those of moderate means would have to bear the shock and the loss. No subsequent prosperity, even if the wildest dreams of our bimetallic visionaries should be realized, could make good the loss to the same parties ; to them it would be absolute and irretrievable. Every man's dollar would be worth only fifty cents—the other half would be lost.

2. Every manufacturer having future contracts to fill at existing prices, that is, prices based on the present purchasing power of the currency, would be hopelessly stricken. While labor and materials would at once advance, the prices of his goods already contracted for would remain the same. He would not only be unable to deliver the goods, but would be liable to an action for damages for failure to fulfil. The law affords no escape from such misfortune. This would destroy a very large part of that most deserving class, the small manufacturers, who have held on during the long depression, "hustling " for contracts even with the narrowest margin

or no profit at all, merely to keep their works going, maintain their credit, and pay their work-people.

3. It would instantly reduce the value of every fire and life insurance policy in the country and require every holder of a policy to take out another of equal value in order to secure equivalent protection for his property or an equal value for the beneficiaries of his forethought. It may be said that less money would be required to effect new insurance, but the probability is that companies would be compelled to raise their rates to a gold standard. Besides this, in many cases further insurance is impossible.

4. It would reduce the value of every deposit in a savings bank or any other banking institution, which would at once become payable in money of half the purchasing power of the present, thereby reducing the value of each depositor's account.

5. It would enable the national banks to realize on all loans a profit equal to half their circulation. As the bonds deposited to secure circulation are payable in gold, they would only have to redeem their issues in the depreciated currency, release their bonds and go out of business, to realize one-half their investment.

6. The man who owes another a debt payable in gold, would thereafter, have not only to pay the actual difference between gold and silver, but the commission of the broker he would have to employ to procure it for him. This would probably not be less than a tenth of one per cent. added to the real cost of exchange.

As all the bonds of states, cities, counties, and corporations and nearly all the mortgages, leases, time loans, and
bank paper of the country are now payable in gold, this
would be a notable loss.   It has been estimated that
we have more than *twenty billion dollars* of debt, of which
at least three-fourths is on gold-contracts.   Every dollar
of this would be enhanced by this difference in value
taken out of the debtor's pocket and transferred to that
of the trafficker in money.

7. The debtor whose obligation does not specify
the kind of currency in which it is to be paid, would, of
course, be benefited by the advance in the apparent
value of what he possesses.   As it would take more dollars to represent the value of what he sold and his
creditor would have to accept them at their present
equivalency, he would be able to realize about half his
debt by such depreciation.   If we leave out bank-ac-
counts, savings-bank deposits, life and fire insurance
policies, and other debts of this character, the amount
of such indebtedness now outstanding, is not very large,
and would be still smaller before such a policy could go
into operation.   Should a president be elected pledged
to free-coinage, every creditor having an over-due obligation not payable in gold, would of course press its
liquidation.   During the months that would intervene
between the election and the installation of such a
party in power, every such debt would be brought to
suit and the debtor compelled to do one of three things :
to wit, pay his debt, suffer execution or foreclosure, or

furnish a new obligation payable in gold. It is, therefore, only the debtor whose obligation might not then be due who could possibly reap advantage from the wholesale depreciation of the established equivalency. The man who would seek to lighten his own burden at the risk of increasing to such an extent as seems in this case inevitable that which others bear, certainly deserves little consideration. If any one has a right to speak as a representative of the debtor class it is the writer of this volume. Dependent upon his own exertions for daily bread ; engaged in an occupation in which both opportunity and compensation are the most precarious ; working habitually more hours a day than any manual laborer ; taking no respite, enjoying no holiday ; suffering from infirmity that leaves few hours free from pain, and bearing a burden of obligation he would gladly give his life to discharge, he surely does not represent any thought, purpose, or inclination inimical to the poorest laborer or prejudicial to the interest of the most sorely beset debtor in all the land. The fact that a man is in debt, however, does not release him from obligation to regard the general welfare, not his own petty opportunity, as the rule of his political action. There can be in a republic, no more dangerous tendency than that which invites men to base their public action upon a hope of relief from their own misfortune through disregard of the rights of others.

8. The owners of silver bullion at the time such a policy should go into effect would be the class who would derive the chief advantage therefrom. There is

no doubt that its value would be somewhat enhanced, even when measured by gold, through its unrestricted coinage and instant certification, since the reduction of the supply thereby produced would naturally advance its price. To what extent if would be increased it is impossible to state. Considering the amount on hand already coined, nearly $400,000,000, the amount of bullion in the government's possession awaiting coinage and the immense surplus of silver in other countries, it does not seem probable that the roseate hopes, even of the present holders of silver, would be very largely realized.

As to the future production of silver, there is little reason to expect that its market value would be greatly enhanced. The dream that the world can be compelled to undertake again the problem of free-coinage of two metals at a fixed ratio of equivalency is evidently futile. A largely increased *restricted* coinage of silver is probably attainable by international agreement ; but the effect of the adoption of a silver standard by the United States would tend still further to restrict its use by European nations, since as soon as our present gold-indebtedness was wiped out, it would diminish the demand for gold as a basis of credit-currency abroad, and leave our stock of that metal free to swell the reserves of European monetary systems, thereby strengthening instead of weakening the gold monometallism of Europe.

That we would reap compensating advantages by securing the trade of the Orient through the adoption of a silver standard of equivalency seems at least doubtful, in view of the ract that England, the only nation, until recent years, to adopt the gold standard, has outstripped all others in securing the trade of the East. The fact should also be remembered that our Chinese Exclusion Acts cut us off from any sympathetic co-operation with the greatest silver nation of the world. On the whole, it may safely be said that the business of silver production is likely to be the only industry to receive advantage, should the policy of free-coinage of silver ever prevail in this country and even this, to a much less extent than is claimed by its advocates.

9. Another matter that should not be lost sight of is the almost irretrievable character of the change to a silver standard of equivalency, if it should happen that the hopes of the advocates of free-coinage should prove delusive. While the change from a double-standard to a single one based on the most valuable coin-metal, if made with care and prudence, does not produce any serious results, can the same be said of a change from silver-monometallism to the gold-standard? The instances of such change are not many, and none of them, it is believed, have been made by peoples approaching ours in recuperative energy. There is every reason to believe that such an experiment would almost wholly destroy our magnificent national credit and leave us to struggle back to a gold basis under an enormous load of debt which we should be compelled to refund at a rate of interest unknown to us as a nation since the most critical period of the war for the union.

10. There is one other view of the probable effect of free-coinage of silver at this time, which, it seems to me, has hitherto been given too little attention. It is beyond question that the election of a president favorable to such policy and having it in his power by a simple executive act to put it in operation even in defiance of a majority of both houses of Congress, would under present financial conditions, create a panic unprecedented even by that which followed the election of 1892. Such panic, like its great predecessor, would be precipitated not so much by actual conditions as by that apprehension which, in the business world, always discounts anticipated disaster. To say that it would cause the utter failure and hopeless insolvency of a larger number of business establishments than did the "crash" of 1892–3, is but to echo the conviction of every thoughtful man. That such failures would be attended with a still further restriction of the area of profitable employment every one knows. Suppose that, after the election in November, the present business depression should be aggravated by such a panic as must inevitably follow the triumph of free-silver—what would be the consequences? Suppose it should add fifty or twenty, or even ten per cent. to the number of the unemployed, and take away, as it surely would, the hope of better times by which so many have so long been buoyed up? Who shall say what scenes we might not witness in our great cities. Want and despair are terrible incentives to violence and insurrection, to riot and bloodshed. Prom-

ises are of no avail to a populace without work, without food, and without reasonable hope of better conditions. From such study of our recent long-continued depression as the writer has been able to make, he is fully satisfied that a period of great financial stringency following the coming election would be attended with such scenes of riot and destruction as have never been witnessed in this country. He has no desire to enact the rôle of alarmist and does not believe the American people will so far lose the capacity for self-government of which we have so long boasted, as to make such a condition possible ; but safety always lies in the clear apprehension of probable consequences. Thanks to the wonderful increase of productive capacity, no man in all the world suffers hunger now save those who from lack of wages may be unable to buy the necessaries of life. But this hunger once aroused and made a general condition is the most terrible monster that can threaten the peace of civilized society.

In all these respects the free-coinage of silver stands in marked contrast as a proposed remedy for existing monetary evils, to the safe, simple, and effective method for securing an abundant and stable currency which this volume is intended to suggest.

11. One more subject remains to be considered There is no doubt a very considerable element of our population, not inferior to any other element in general intelligence, moral worth, and patriotic purpose, who look with serious apprehension upon the tendency of wealth

8

to concentrate in few hands, to the establishment of
class-distinctions based on wealth alone, and the increase
of dependency that results from the centralization of
business in a constantly decreasing number of great establishments rather than in an increasing number of
small ones. That such a tendency is to be deplored no
man can question. The concentration of power, whether
physical, political, or financial, in few hands is always
dangerous. That means will be found to counteract this
tendency in the future there is no doubt. At present,
knowledge of the extent and causes of such tendency is
lacking. Imagination and vague hypothesis have been
too frequent elements of speculation upon the subject.
With fuller knowledge is sure to come a better comprehension of the remedies required.

That a very considerable proportion of those whose
apprehension of malign conditions as the result of this tendency is most intense, are inclined to venture the experiment of free-coinage of silver as a remedy therefor, every
one who has given any attention to the subject very well
knows. The writer does not need to state here that he
has a most ardent sympathy with those who entertain the
most serious apprehension for the results of this growing
tendency. Grave as is his apprehension of evil consequences to result from the adoption of the silver standard
of equivalency, he might even feel constrained to give it
his support as an alternative evil, were there reasonable
ground to believe that it would prove a remedy for this
tendency. He has given many years to the study

of these questions, and while rarely able to approve the drastic remedies proposed by reformers who are not willing to see evils cured by the same slow process of growth by which they are evolved, he has no less doubt of the need of cure and perhaps much greater hope of the ultimate betterment of harsh conditions.

In the present case, his opposition to the free-coinage of silver is based not only upon the views heretofore set forth, but on an abiding conviction that it would·directly and powerfully tend to increase the proportional area of dependency and enhance the tendency toward the concentration of values in few hands—in other words, to make the rich relatively richer, and to increase the number of the poor even if it did not accentuate the conditions of the poorest.

Without discussing the matter at any length he desires to state a few propositions on which his conviction rests, that the effect of free-coinage would be exactly the converse of what the class referred to hope and desire it might be.   These propositions are :

Any depreciation of general values must fall most heavily upon that class who stand just above those who are dependent solely upon to-day's labor for to-morrow's bread.   This class is composed in the first place of self-employers, mechanics, tradesmen, and the like, who have by thrift and industry acquired a little surplus and have invested the same in business which requires their own labor and that of a few others.   The destruction of such a business not only throws these wage-earners out of employment, but precipitates the employer and his family into the class of absolutely dependent laborers, thereby increasing its numbers and decreasing the opportunities of those already in its ranks.

Financial convulsions have been among the chief causes of the concentration of wealth in few hands. The strong survive : the weak are crushed. When the storm is over there are fewer rich men and more poor men than when it begun. Also, the rich are relatively richer than they were ; and the poor relatively poorer, not only in purse but in opportunity. The failure of a great merchant or manufacturer may for a time lower the price of goods by throwing his stock upon the market, but it will cause the failure of a dozen, perhaps a hundred, others whose wealth will be absorbed by other rich men, while those who fail and their families are added to the ranks of dependency.

Suppose the greatest estate in the country should to-morrow become insolvent, by whom would its $200,000,-000 of values be absorbed? By other men already worth millions. Its insolvency would drag down many others whose possessions would also go into the hands of great capitalists. There would be a hundred or a thousand more poor men as a result, while the number of the very rich would be reduced to a like extent ; but the rich men who were left would own all that the greater number had owned before.

A few great farmers may be compelled by financial stringency to sell their lands ; but ten times as many small ones will lose theirs and become homeless renters or dependent laborers.   Because of these things, stability of values and general prosperity are essential conditions of all successful effort toward the cure of this tendency.

That free-silver would cause a financial panic no man can doubt, and if so its effects on the comparative distribution of wealth would be harmful just in proportion to the extent and duration of such monetary crisis. For this reason, if for no other, the writer would be compelled to oppose this policy, and for this reason he feels compelled to invite attention to the fact that the plan for the improvement of the currency, outlined herein, could not possibly result in any disturbance of values nor benefit one class of society at the cost of any other class —would cast no man down and lift no man up, but open the gate of opportunity for all.

XIV

CURRENCY AND PROTECTION.

THIS volume was written for suggestion, not controversy. The author was impressed with the belief that
the apparent issues of the pending political contest were
obscuring the real questions to be decided, thereby nar-
rowing the range of discussion to a controversy solely
as to the abstract merits of two theories of coinage, to
the neglect of our financial condition and the use of our
national credit to supply a currency well calculated to
meet the desires of all except those who may have a personal interest either in the free-coinage of silver or the
substitution for our present credit-money of a currency
consisting of bank-issues based on national bonds.

Of course, the silver mine owner and those otherwise
engaged in the production of this metal have a personal
interest in the adoption of a policy of unrestricted coinage,
which very naturally tends to bias their view of the public interest. This fact involves no derogation of the
character or worth of such citizens—it is merely a
statement of the universal law of human nature :

> " When self the wavering balance holds
> 'Tis rarely right adjusted."

The same condition is found on the other side of the question. The capitalist who desires a good investment ; the broker whose harvest-time comes when there is a need for a particular kind of currency, and the banker who under such a system would enjoy the benefit of an immense loan of public credit—all these are equally interested in the profits to be derived from the only system hitherto suggested instead of free-silver. The judgment of one of these classes is just as likely to be biassed as that of the other, and neither of them can be accepted as wholly free from suspicion.

The author's purpose, in the plan set forth, has been to suggest a form of currency which should meet both extremes of popular thought and give :

1. A currency as abundant as may be desired, and

2. A currency of unquestionable stability which shall at all times be *as good as gold*.

He has endeavored to unite with these qualities the following desirable conditions, to wit :

1. A great reduction of the interest-charge in comparison with an equivalent amount of bond-indebtedness requisite as a basis for a like amount of bank-currency.

2. The avoidance of special favor to any class or institution so that the advantage resulting from the issue of currency would accrue equally to all holders of the same.

The bank of issue, however valuable it may have been in the past, is a fact not in full accord with modern tendencies. Dependent upon legislation as its issues must always be for desirability and stability, it bears always the complexion of monopoly and favor to a specific class. Especially is this true since modern history has developed the fact that such issues can only be made stable by having the legal-tender quality attached to them and their credit enhanced by the guaranty of government. It may well be doubted whether a great central bank like those of the leading nations of Europe, or even one formed on the plan of our present national banks, is in harmony with our institutions. The overthrow of the old Bank of the United States was in its day a great financial calamity, but there are few who do not now believe that it was a national blessing. The power of segregated capital is serious enough without the aid of governmental favor or the control of the credit-currency of the country.

Much has been said in opposition to the idea of the government being engaged in banking. There is much ground for this objection so long as the currency it issues is maintained on the theory of " constant redeemability " which compels it not only to issue currency but to engage in brokerage, and that, too, upon essentially unequal and unfavorable terms. The business of banking is for the profit of the banker. He does not engage to issue currency except for profit, and no man has any right to demand that any particular policy be adopted for his especial advantage. Currency is the business of government, and the advantage resulting from the issue of credit-money, whatever its form, should accrue not to bankers as a class, but to all the people.

As has been shown, the credit of the country may be easily, safely, and most profitably used as currency by uniting the desirability of the bond with the denominational character of our existing demand-obligations. It is possible that even a lower rate of interest than that suggested might ultimately be adopted. Even at that rate, however, it is a much cheaper currency than can be obtained by any other means by which assured stability can be secured—less than one-fourth the cost of our present bank-notes and unquestionably cheaper than the legal-tender notes of the Bank of England, the price of whose shares is the measure of it profits, a large portion of which depend on its use of the public credit and control of the public funds.

Whether the particular plan suggested in this work shall be adopted or not is a matter of no moment. The writer's purpose is to direct attention to the fact that abundance and stability of the currency may be attained and an immense economy in the administration and liquidation of the public debt secured by abandoning the theory of " constant redeemability " and substituting periodicity of payment of interest and a fixed and gradual liquidation. What shall take its place after the volume of the public debt has been reduced below the limit required for currency circulation may well be left to time to determine.

One thing should by no means be neglected : the whole or some fixed part of the duties on imports should be paid in gold. When a government engages to pay the principal and interest of its debt in gold, it should make such legislative provisions as will show to every creditor its purpose and ability to redeem such pledge. Unless it has the evident power to *demand gold payments* on at least a portion of its revenue charges, no man can ever be sure that it will have gold in its treasury to meet such obligations whether they be great or small.

Another motive which influenced the writer in the preparation of this work was an earnest desire to invite the attention of the Republican party to the intimate and vital relation that exists between the currency question and the economic policy of protection. A most earnest believer in the economic doctrine of protection, especially as applied to our present industrial conditions, particularly when co-ordinated with the related principles reciprocity and preferential duties on importations made in American bottoms, there seemed to him a tendency to regard protection as the sole function of government and the only thing necessary to insure the immediate restoration of old-time conditions of prosperity—high prices, uniform profits, and phenomenal opportunity. The truth is, that over-production and the surplus of labor resulting from the industrial development of the past have brought a new epoch, one in which the economics of production are bound to constitute a more important feature of our industrial conditions than ever before.

Because of this fact the question of an abundant and stable currency united with a marked diminution of the cost of our public debt, now approaching again the sum of *two billion dollars*, becomes a matter of vital importance to the success of protection in securing the results anticipated from its re-application to our industrial conditions. When some months ago the writer ventured the prediction that the currency question would prove "the hot end of the poker in the coming campaign," the idea was greeted with open ridicule by many of his party associates for whose opinions he has always entertained the very highest respect. That the result has fully justified his expectation is a matter of little gratification, since it has found the Republican party wholly unprepared with a distincive policy beyond the mere negative declaration against free-silver and the peril of a change of the standard of equivalency at this time. To the question how the existing evils of our monetary system are to bé remedied it makes no answer nor any authoritative suggestion.

Yet it must be apparent to all that, under existing conditions, protection without a stable and abundant currency and the adoption of effective means for the protection of the public credit is simply an eagle without wings. Its efficacy as an economic system depends wholly on such restoration of confidence as will incline capital to engage in, to support and back productive enterprise. This confidence is in a superlative degree dependent on a currency which not only commands popular approval but which itself does not offer an inviting field for speculative investment, and thereby tend to withdraw capital from productive investment. This is a

great detect of all banking-currency. Under our present system every dollar of bank-currency requires the
investment of a like amount in bonds, so that there can
be no real enhancement of the circulation but only a
change of form. Indeed, there is some restriction, since
every bank is required not only to keep bonds on deposit but to maintain a specific reserve for the redemption of its own notes. This becomes important as
affecting not the essential character of protection as a
national policy but its probable efficacy at this time.

Protection has practically come to be an admitted
necessity. While the majority of those who are theo-
retical believers in what is termed free-trade as an
universal economic principle, have not, of course, sur-
rendered that belief, a continually increasing deficit, due
in part to lack of revenue and in part to drain upon
the treasury caused by the conditions of the currency,
have satisfied every candid and patriotic mind that something must be done to increase the revenues ; and, under
existing conditions, even the free-trader is bound to ad-
mit that there is no other course to pursue but to try
again the policy of protection. For these reasons, protection has practically dropped out of the campaign
as a contested principle, and the American people are
turning their attention to the currency problem with a
universality of interest never before manifested in any
political issue since that involved in the struggle for the
preservation of national unity was decided. This volume is in part intended, therefore, to supply an apparent

defect, in the Republican position and show that the evils of our present monetary and financial conditions may be easily, cheaply, and certainly cured without modification of the existing standard of equivalency, whether by adopting the plan outlined herein or one which may commend itself to the general approval as better—to show, indeed, that it is unnecessary to appeal to the dangerous expedient of unrestricted coinage of silver to secure the monetary conditions desired by all, abundance and stability of the currency and absolute uniformity of value between all its parts.

XV.

THE RICH AND THE POOR.

THE author was especially impelled to put forth this volume by a very serious apprehension in regard to the consequences to flow from an apparently increasing antagonism between two classes, or rather two conditions of American life. By this is meant that moral and intellectual condition of contrasted elements of our people which is popularly known as the "war between labor and capital," the "conflict between the rich and the poor," "between the debtor and the creditor classes." These phrases, quoted from the very highest authority, are used to designate a spirit or tendency not easily definable, yet in a general way universally understood. To the author's mind they represent a most dangerous and deplorable tendency. While it is possible that under certain circumstances, like those which preceded that terrible social and political convulsion which we term the "French Revolution," conflict between two phases of society seems unavoidable, he does not believe that any such condition exists or is likely to arise between economic classes of American society. The rich man of to-day is the result of antecedent conditions for which he is no more responsible than his neighbor of moderate means, and the debtor is such by his own volition and can by no means blame his creditor for the failure of his own expectations. The restoration of prosperity must depend upon harmonious co-operation between these classes rather than in a conflict which unsettles values, paralyzes production, destroys the confidence in assured profit for the one, and closes the door of opportunity to the other.

There are, of course, exceptions to every general rule and especially to vague classifications of society, but as a rule it may safely and justly be said that nothing can compare with the elastic hopefulness of the American debtor unless it be the patient forbearance and cheerful helpfulness of the American creditor. Together they make the strongest and most harmonious economic combination of co-ordinate financial forces which the world has ever known. The marvellous industrial and financial progress of the Republic during the past thirty years, has been due in the main, to their harmonious co-operation. In no other country has capital been so favorable to enterprise ; in no other country has enterprise so lavishly rewarded capital. The improvement of economic conditions in the future will not lie along the line of conflict between these forces, but along that of substantial agreement. The true interest of capital lies in the road to general prosperity, to general employment, to general comfort and general success.

For a time, tendencies may favor concentration of wealth and restriction of opportunity; but such tendencies must steadily relax before competition and the irrepressible aspiration of the American people.   In this country the time is sure to come, as it has already come in Switzerland, when the more wealthy element of a population, strangely imbued with an almost universal desire for the betterment of general conditions, shall vie with, even if it does not excel, the laboring class and those of restricted means in *the desire to ameliorate our general industrial and financial conditions.*

There are, no doubt, very many of this class who are not now animated by such purpose.   This is but natural. The struggle for predominance whether financial or political always diverts attention and sympathy from popular needs and existing tendencies.   The politician whose attention has been long absorbed by the strife of parties, and the millionaire whose utmost powers have been engaged in the strife for wealth, are both unfitted to make a fair estimate of the general need, the general aspiration, the aggregated tendency of any particular time. So, too, is the man whose energies have for a lifetime been absorbed by the strife for daily bread.   His views are narrowed to his own wants, his own comforts, his own immediate advantage.   Improved conditions will never result from heated strife between these elements.   It is in vain that the employer declares that his interests are identical with those of the laborer, and equally vain for the laborer to assert that his employer is his enemy.

To a certain point their interests are identical ; beyond that they diverge. The remedy is not to be found in heated conflict resulting in still further divergence of sentiment and sympathy, but in the cultivation of closer relations and a fuller comprehension of the needs of each and the ultimate welfare of all—in mutual co-operation rather than in mutually destructive antagonism. The war between rich and poor must be waged with light and knowledge which shall show the common peril of existing tendencies and unite the better elements of both great classes in a common sentiment which shall constitute a public opinion making the " general welfare" rather than the specific interests of either class the basis of political action.

Such changes are the result of growth, not of instant revolution. The accumulation of so great a proportion of wealth in a few hands has been the result of tendencies as old as civilization—of conditions many of which antedate our national existence. These have been greatly modified in the recent past and are destined to even greater modification in the near future. For this every good citizen should hope ; this result all good men and women should prepare themselves to promote in any of the thousand peaceful and kindly ways in which influence may be exerted on others ; for this condition every one should wait, as a thing worth waiting for, with patience. Because of this, the man who seeks to precipitate a state of war between rich and poor, who seeks to promote and intensify a sentiment of injustice and oppression which economic and industrial conditions may have engendered, who would stir the debtor to resentment and thereby move the creditor to resulting animosity ; the man or the party that does these things, whatever the motive that may be proclaimed, whether sincere or insincere in purpose —such a man or such a party is not only dangerous to national prosperity, but a threat to the future of civilization.

Methods and theories are of little importance. The world pays little heed to them or to those who formulate them. It never follows in the path marked out for it by the wise. Those who are able to declare with the utmost positiveness the methods of the future—they and their schemes are soon forgotten. The wisdom of the wisest of to-day who would put fetters on to-morrow and seek to establish with the force of compulsory legislation a new condition, whose beneficence is a matter of theory rather than popular tendency, is nearly always folly. But the aspiration of the weak, the purpose of the many, that shapes itself slowly but surely into new methods, is the only secure hope of improved conditions and the highest prosperity.

THE END.